Fly-fishing for IRISH TROUT

Also by Niall Fallon:
The Armada in Ireland

Fly-fishing for IRISH TROUT

Niall Fallon

RB

Roberts' Books, Kilkenny, Ireland

To Leo Maher,
my angling uncle

Published in the Republic of Ireland by
Roberts' Books, St. Kieran Street,
Kilkenny, Co. Kilkenny,
Republic of Ireland, Tel. 0409 5054

Also published by Roberts' Books:
The History and Antiquities of the Diocese of Ossory — 4 vols.
    by Rev. Canon Carrigan
History of the Queen's County — 2 vols. by Rev. Canon O'Hanlon
History of the Ely O'Carroll Territory by Rev. John Gleeson
The History of Clonmel by Rev. Wm. P. Canon Burke

Fallon, Niall
Fly fishing for Irish trout.
1. Trout fishing — Ireland
2. Fly fishing
I. Title
799.1'755   SH687
ISBN 0-907561-11-X

Printed in the Republic of Ireland by
Mount Salus Press, Tritonville Road, Sandymount, Dublin 4.

CONTENTS

CONTENTS

CONTENTS

ACKNOWLEDGEMENTS

Anglers, as always, have been generous with advice; my thanks to the many and varied of them who spoke on river-bank and loch; to my wife, a non-angler but now fully resigned to my condition; Morrough Linnane, a constant companion; three angling brothers, Matthew, Tom and James Fort; Stephen Lewis; Harry and June Hodgson of Currarevagh in Connemara, an incomparable fishing hotel; the Holden-Hindlays of Cumbria; the Hellyers in Yorkshire; and the Gibson-Brabazons of Westmeath for many kindnesses.

A special gratitude is due to Dick (J. R.) Harris, who went to endless trouble to solve a few of my fly-tying problems; to Bord Fáilte (the Irish Tourist Board), generous in so many ways over the years; the National Library in Dublin, with a splendid and enviable collection of Irish angling books; to the Central Fisheries Board for much useful information; and to the many anglers, book-collectors, enthusiasts and libraries who lent me material. To these and others my inadequate thanks.

PREFACE

The brown trout, that perfected and natural design of grace and beauty, surely personifies the apogée of any trout-angler's imagination. A wonderful creature in a wondrous environment, of whose complex pattern he is just one small part; and an expression too, of the illumination of natural things and their mysterious and continued regeneration.

Angling involves the angler in another, if small and more obtrusive part of the same pattern, for which we, as anglers, can only be grateful.

This book, which I believe to be the first to deal with Irish trout-fishing in such detail, will cast little light for those who fish for trout other than with fly. It comes partly from wanting to communicate the little of real use I have learned about fly-fishing and partly too, from the curious fact that whereas much has been written about Irish fishing, no comprehensive work exists which covers fly-fishing for trout in Ireland. If this book fills the gap and if, while reading it, an angler nods and says "yes, that's true", then I will be happy enough.

I have tried not to be too definitive, since trout angling defies such. No fish can break a rigid rule so arrogantly and with such finality. My methods have worked for me over some 35 years' fishing, during which I have been lucky enough to fish in all the 32 counties of this island.

No angler can cover a whole country — nor indeed should he write about waters he has not fished. So there are gaps here and there, to my regret. It remains one of the great pleasures of anticipation that they remain to be filled. And for that, and for the unequalled delight which trout fishing has given me, I am grateful.

County Meath,
September 1983

Brown trout of six pounds, eight ounces, caught by the author. The fish took a Green Peter sedge fished dry on an Irish midland lake and took almost twenty minutes to subdue in total darkness. Today it stands mounted on a wall in the author's study — the biggest trout he has yet caught. The full story of its capture appears in Chapter Four, "Evening Lake Angling".

Chapter One

The Changing Scene

Irish trout angling today and yesterday — what others thought —
decline and fall — a warning — signs of hope — conservation

Fishing, if I, a fisher, may protest,
Of pleasures the sweetest, of sports the best;
Of exercises the most excellent;
Of recreations the most innocent;
But now the sport is marde, and wott ye why?
Fishes decrease and fishers multiply.

Thomas Bastard

As it is everywhere, trout angling in Ireland has changed much
and is changing yet. On balance it is not nearly so good as it
was say, a century ago; or even a half century ago. But it is still
of a high overall quality.

What the trout angler of today would give for Irish trout angling
of former years! At one time, few rivers were fished by anyone other
than the local man; for the rest, the bulk of the fishing was done on
the great lakes of the midlands limestone plain and of the west.
Salmon ruled lordly over the trout. The dry-fly, now so familiar (and
getting more so) was a rarity, even a heresy. With little or no
pollution, precious little angling pressure and ideal conditions for
breeding fish, the Irish trout lived a decidedly more pleasurable life
than he does today.

Although the literature of Irish trout angling is a poor thing indeed
to that which has attended the fat English trout of Test and Itchen,
we have been given enough glimpses of its past to savour even a little
its marvellous flavour. That good angling doctor, W. A. Peard, who
spent an entire season moving his domestic entourage from excellent
water to excellent water, wrote almost nonchalantly of trout angling
in the midlands which, read today, yields little to imagination. Trout
of up to eight or ten pounds were common; a day's catch was deemed
poor if several at least of its captives were not over four or five

1

pounds. The average day's haul indeed, would be a lifetime's
ambition for today's average trout angler if we are to believe all that
Peard wrote — and he was, by all accounts, a sound and honest man.

W. H. Maxwell, who made immortal in *Wild Sports of the West* that
still-fine salmon river, the Owenduff in wildest Mayo, made
astounding catches of white trout and salmon — but we talk not of
salmon here. We can believe him. Less reliable perhaps is
Cosmopolite, otherwise R. Allen, whose catches often touched the
incredible and whose recording of them even more so. Dividing both
by a considerable factor, however, still leaves us with a smather of
envy.

The nineteenth century, in hindsight, may well have been the
apogée of Irish trout angling. O'Gorman, in his *The Practice of
Angling*, published twice in mid-century (which shows at least a
healthy following for the sport) was its first scientifically-inclined
recorder; and while much of that remarkable book is primarily
philosophical, it contains a positive wealth of useful insight on
angling and its methods a century and more ago. It confirms, if we
need confirmation, the consistently high standard of trout angling.
Add to your reading of O'Gorman, Peard, Maxwell and
Cosmopolite the less detailed work of Belton, Newlands and
Bickerdyke and the picture is rounded out even more.

But it is not yet complete. We have purposely left until last, like the
last and biggest trout of the day which launches itself upon our sedge
at the last cast of the evening, the delightful companionship of one
Gregory Greendrake. This pseudonymous masking of the more
prosaically-named J. Coad wrote what must be the Irish angling
classic — *The Angling Excursions of Gregory Greendrake in the Counties of
Wicklow, Meath, Westmeath, Longford and Cavan* in 1832. It was, and
remains so, sparklingly amusing and informative, most of all to the
midland angler. Its classicism is matched by one of its principal
characters — that great and unique Irish tying, the Golden Olive,
the seminal imitation of the lake olive. It is said to have originated on
the waters of Lough Glore, near Castlepollard in County
Westmeath; as I write, an oil portrait of that water hangs opposite
me. And I can see, in its blue waters, the roll of a great trout one
September evening as he came at — and missed — my silver sedge.
I quake still. He was closer to three feet long than two. His weight I
cannot bring myself to guess at.

But by the beginning of this century, the Greendrake days were
ended. The rise was over. The picture since then is one of decline,
occasionally fast, occasionally barely seen; but decline nonetheless.

I have no wish to be gloomy. All waters have their good times and bad. Nature is a curious and capricious overseer of the pattern of life; and even our scientists, who grow more scientific each year, cannot pin strict reason on why trout fishing, all visible reasons set aside, is so variable from year to year, from decade to decade, from generation to generation.

That said, this century too, has seen fine trout angling in Ireland. For instance, I have in my desk tape recordings of several of the great ghillies of the western lakes. One, long since dead, recalls the capture in one week of two trout to his rod, the one weighing 21 lbs., the second close on 24 lbs. They were, he said, caught on fly. I have no doubt they were not. But if his memory was at fault, was it equally so when he remembered frequent catches to a boat with two and sometimes three rods fishing of four, five and even six dozen fish weighing between a pound and five pounds?

Let me too, tell you of another ghillie, alive in this year of writing; blinded, in his eighties, yet upright still, and powerful. You needed to be when you rowed eight or sometimes ten hours a day, often in storm and gale. His two best days as ghillie both yielded catches of over 100 trout to three rods, one of them a dapping rod. He had, he said, become more tired landing trout in the net than pulling an oar. Old memories play tricks with themselves; but blank days were few and a typical day's catch would be at least four or six trout to a rod. And all wild Irish trout.

This century, which has seen most of the decline, has seen too, in compensation almost, some of the better writers. If Gregory Greendrake and O'Gorman have cast a longer line than their writer colleagues, to form a clumsy simile, they have had their counterparts after their deaths. T. C. Kingsmill Moore, judge, fly-inventor and tier, angling theorist and humanitarian, laments the passing of the better days in *A Man May Fish*. If you have read it, I need say no more. It is one of the classics of angling literature anywhere. If you have not read it, hasten to do so; it marries delightfully the many disparities of theory, practice, philosophy and experience. And its portrait of Jamesie, the Corrib ghillie, is a lesson in one human observing — and loving — another. Its particular strength is its section — half the book about — on white trout angling in Ireland, of which no more should be said than that anyone who fishes for white trout anywhere and who has not read it has diminished chances of success.

One of the frequent oddities of angling is its attraction for men of thought (oddity perhaps to those outside angling!) A pace behind

Kingsmill Moore but nonetheless a staunch and essential member of the A team of Irish angling chroniclers is Professor A. A. Luce. His *Fishing and Thinking* is just that — a delightful if incomplete vision of one man's marriage of lifelong passion and angling.

I see — again — that I have slipped away to cast over another pool I had meant to leave well alone. Both Kingsmill Moore and Luce, in their different ways, underline the falling-away in Irish trout angling; they recognised it, mourned for it, did what they could and passed on to us the duty of improving it. That they enjoyed better fishing than we have or will have is I think, indisputable. So too did F. D. Barker in his entrancing *An Angler's Paradise*, an Eden he sought to conceal (like many an angler since) by giving its lakes and rivers fictitious names. It is an open secret that the fishing he so enjoyed was in the lakes around Corofin in County Clare, Lough Inchiquin amongst them. Today you may catch trout on Inchiquin as he did sixty or so years ago; but it is a far cry indeed from paradise.

There have been other writers this century — Stephen Gwynn, Gaffey, Corrigeen (Adams), Hi-Regan (J. J. Dunne), Luard, Drought, even the great purist F. M. Halford — who have written on Irish trout angling. From their books, and those of others such as T. J. Hanna, possibly the greatest of Irish fly-tiers, emerge two conclusions — one, that Irish trout angling was then much better than it is today, and second, that many trout waters remained almost unfished and that even those which were fished had nothing like so many anglers as today throng our waters.

I am slipping, as I did not mean to, into sadness for the great past. But it must be said that our forefathers enjoyed a quality of angling which today is equalled only in the remoter outposts of the world, such as Alaska. Irish angling was, without a shadow of doubt, superb. That day is gone, equally without doubt.

And what are we left with?

Despite it all — the pollution, the pressure, the drainage, the poaching — Ireland is still a land of trout water. The trout are smaller, fewer and harder to catch. No longer are they totally wild fish; the age of the stockie is increasingly with us. But overall, there is real quality yet in Irish trout angling; there is plenty of good water. And above all, there is an awareness by a younger and more educated people that not alone can angling be improved but that water is no longer an illimitable and unspoilable heritage.

By nature, anglers are optimistic. How else, why else, would we spend days, even weeks, without a fish? It is easy to throw hands in the air and fishing waters to the wolves. It has happened. In the last

Dapping the traditional way; a favoured method of trout-fishing in the west of Ireland, here used in the expert hands of Connemara ghillie Paddy Clancy of Oughterard, County Galway, fishing on Lough Corrib.

decade, Ireland has lost perhaps its two single finest trout lakes. One of them — Lough Ennell in the midlands — has been restored to life; today trout live and are caught in its once more clear waters. Lough Sheelin in County Cavan is deeply eutrophic, enriched to death's door by excess phosphorus seeping into its waters through the spreading of pig slurry from the intensive pig-farming units around it. It may or may not recover.

These two lakes are a warning. No-one set out deliberately to pollute them. A combination of incredible — truly incredible — official neglect and buck-passing, combined with ignorance and faint-heartedness, led directly to the state in which they found — and to some extent still find — themselves. This in spite of the fact that Ireland has a comprehensive and potentially effective set of anti-pollution laws. Those laws, to a large and alarming degree, have not been and are not being implemented. And because people see quickly that offences can be gotten away with, they are all the more quick to commit them.

The restoration of Lough Ennell is in some ways an encouragement. A decade ago it was dead. Fishing stopped. Last year I stood on the slight slope of Lilliput and watched 27 boats fish the bay which had not seen anglers for many years. They were catching fish. Ennell lived — and lives — again. But it has been lucky. Will others be as lucky?

Lakes can in one sense take less abuse than rivers. They are slow to slough themselves of pollution. Sheelin's waters take a full six months to change fully. Rivers are faster and run downhill, bearing whatever pollutes them with the current. Temporary river pollution is quickly swept away and although it may well kill anything that moves, if not repeated life returns. It is this ability to overcome and renew which sustains many Irish rivers — not the fact that they are polluted. They are, to an alarming extent; and in many ways are worse off than lakes because of this.

But pollution of whatever sort is not the major problem which Irish fishing rivers face. Ireland is a wet and for the most part, low-lying country. Traditionally, many of its rivers flood during the winter and spring, inundating many thousands of acres of lowland. For many years, determined drainage schemes have been carried out by the Board of Works, schemes which have left many once-entrancing rivers looking like deep drains. It has been said that drainage work canalises a river; this is an insult to the often beautiful canal. Drainage work ruins and wrecks a river. It takes away the weeds, that essential environment without which little organic life is possible. It hastens flow and run-off, leaving rivers mere trickles in summer weather, with not enough water to cover a parr's back.

It also makes some rivers almost impossible to fish. The primary purpose of such drainage schemes is to reclaim and make permanently dry any land which in winter has hitherto been useless. Anglers recognise this as being in most cases worthy and essential work. But too many drainage schemes have been carried out with a disregard for anglers, naturalists and conservationists which is no different from a bland contempt. There is no need to wreck a river while draining it — and this has not yet been learned.

Remarkably, rivers do recover from such mauling and raping. In limestone areas, where growth is rich and life determined, in a few years silt will gather, weeds take root, trees fall, boulders tumble down the high banks, cattle tread down banks and watering places — and slowly a river has life again, running and gliding, eddying in deep pools, flattening and racing through gravelly shallows. The trout return. The fly-life begins and thickens. And a river is reborn.

It is encouragement, if small, to see the slow growth of conservation in Ireland. The country's marvellous richness of waters is seen more and more not alone as being threatened, but as being finite and even frail. For too many years anglers stood alone in fighting against depredations of every sort, becoming known in that fight as cranks and even troublemakers. Today they are being joined by others conscious that water is a delicate and rare blessing needing care and protection. Trout angling is just one additional blessing that water brings.

—————— o ——————

SECTION ONE

—————— o ——————

Brown Trout in Lakes

———————————————————— O ————————————————————

(FACING PAGE 6)
Dapping with the natural mayfly, this angler has just landed a superbly-con-ditioned wild brown trout from Lough Ennell in County Westmeath. Formerly and arguably the finest brown trout lake in Ireland, Ennell was drastically pol-luted some years ago but is now slowly recovering. At one time it offered prob-ably the finest mayfly fishing in these islands.

(OPPOSITE)
A good catch of five brown trout from Lough Inchiquin in County Clare. Still a fine angling lake, the alkaline Inchiquin has nonetheless declined steeply from its excellence of half a century ago when F. D. Barker immortalised it and its neigh-bouring lakes around Corofin in the Irish angling classic, "An Angler's Paradise".

(ON PAGE 8)
A map showing the principal brown trout waters in Ireland. The three boxed areas denote the principal groups of limestone lakes which give the best lake ang-ling, while the main river systems are also shown. For closer study, anglers should look at the large-scale Ordnance Survey maps of each area.

BROWN TROUT WATERS
(RIVERS AND LAKES)

0 SCALE   20   40   MILES 60

PRINCIPAL LIMESTONE LAKES
A; L.Conn, L Cullen
B; L.Corrib; L.Mask
C; L.Carra; L. Arrow
D: Ls.Ennell, Owel, Derravarragh,
   Sheelin, Glore, White Lake

Chapter Two

Brown Trout in Lakes

The three types of lakes — the limestone lakes — the angling year —
table of natural fly and matching artificial — when best to fish

---

Bring the rod, the line, the reel!
Bring, oh bring, the osier creel!
Bring me flies of fifty kinds,
Bring me showers and clouds and winds!

Thomas Todd Stoddart

Look at the map of Ireland on the opposite page and the
abundance of water leaps out. So much of it is there that anglers
coming to fish in Ireland for the first time voice a near-common
surprise that not alone is there so much trout water but that much of
it is more or less free.

Whilst trout rivers have been distributed with a discriminatory
fairness in this land of water, the hand which broadcast flowing
water so liberally has been harsher on stillwaters. With a few
exceptions, the best of the lake angling is in the midlands and the
west and in turn the best of that is over the limestone beds which lie
underneath so much of the Irish countryside. Outside those areas,
lake angling declines.

Irish lakes can be put roughly into three categories: (a) the great
limestone lakes of the midlands and west; (b) smaller limestone lakes
around the country, and (c) non-limestone lakes, medium-sized and
small.

There is not a great deal more that anyone can say about the first
category. It comprises Corrib, Mask, Conn, Cullen, Arrow and five
or six others. The names are world-famous and the lakes have
deserved that. That they are no longer nearly so good as they were is
a fact. But they still hold great quantities of trout, good trout and for
the most part provide free fishing.

The smaller limestone lakes offer an interesting and indeed
challenging contrast, for it is here that the qualified expansion in

Irish lake angling will, I think, come. Broadly speaking, the trout angling in these smaller lakes is undeveloped and often almost absent. Coarse fish, particularly pike and perch, rule the roost.

Because the better-known waters of Corrib and Mask and their kin have been available, these smaller waters have been neglected. On the whole, they are relatively unpolluted and unfished. With proper development, they could become first-class fisheries, with the inestimable benefit of being manageable, largely because of their size and controllability.

As you might imagine, improving and controlling the fishing on Corrib's 68 square miles is clearly beyond the modest capability of any angling-based organisation and there must be considerable doubt as to the value of stocking these bigger lakes so long as there is no machinery capable adequately of preventing abuses by anglers and others, and indeed of preventing pollution and other hazards.

The third category comprises those lakes which will always be with us — small, usually acidic lakes, often in hills or mountains, with few coarse fish and large stocks of small, even under-sized trout, with poor feeding. They are fairly plentifully and evenly distributed around Ireland and occasionally are the only trout fishing available in an area.

That, broadly, is the picture of Irish lake angling for brown trout. What of its quality?

I have written already, in the previous chapter, of how this has declined. In some instances, such as Sheelin and Ennell, the cause is clear — pollution. In others, such as Mask, it is far less clear. These days, when competitions are held on Mask, stock fish have to be put in if reasonable returns are to be made. Attend a weigh-in at the end of a "national" and the most of the fish will be a pound or under, as alike as two peas, often with deformed fins — clear signs of stockies.

And yet Mask is full of trout, wild trout. On some days, the fortunate days, you will see such a rise of fish as to cause you to rub your eyes. Great fish, big fish, wild fish. yet they are not caught in any quantity. Some factor, so far unknown, has caused them to turn away from the angler's fly. Much the same can be said of Corrib where I once witnessed a rise of fish, on a still July evening, so heavy that in almost every square yard of water over a large area a trout was rising, feeding on a heavy hatch of sedges. The lake was full of fish. Yet they too, are hard to catch and it is to the stockie, more and more, that anglers look for their catches.

The midland lakes are similar, Owel, near the geographical centre of Ireland, is under heavy pressure from Dublin anglers particularly and must be stocked to satisfy them. Yet it has plenty of wild fish; but they are devilishly hard to catch. Not so the stockie, who has become an easy target in his first few days of freedom. Many are the tales of greedy anglers taking forty, fifty and even sixty of these fish in a day where the bag limit is six to ten fish. How can you have good angling, even based on stock fish, if anglers behave thus?

The most popular theory as to why wild trout are harder to catch is that the rich feeding on the limestone bottoms has been restored to them by the elimination of pike through the activities in these waters of the former Inland Fisheries Trust, now the Central Fisheries Board. This theory holds that when many pike were present, the trout was forced largely to the surface to look for its food. All we can say is that there is no affirmatory evidence one way or the other. I suspect myself that taking pike from a water means more but smaller trout and little more than that.

The angling year

Theoretically you can fish for trout in Ireland from February 15th to the middle of October — seven and a half months, a more than generous allowance, provided you are willing to move to take advantage of earlier and later closing times in different regions.

Few anglers do that however. February, March and half of April are usually the worst months of the Irish winter. Indeed they *are* the Irish winter, filled with rain, frost, storm and flood. They are also cold and blustery, fit only for the hardy angler.

They do though, offer occasionally excellent fishing. Trout even in February are sometimes — though not always — in surprisingly good condition, particularly if the winter has been mildish. They are hungry and take the fly well. But more often than not they are not in the best of health and need the rich feeding of later April and May to bring them into fighting trim.

St. Patrick's Day on March 17th often traditionally marks the actual start of the lake angler's year. On the whole, it is a satisfactory date; the trout are largely recovered from their winter rigours, the weather is getting milder, some fly is on the water. There is, all in all, something to be said for starting the season on that date.

The wise angler, beginning his season towards the end of March, will base his angling on the natural fly then hatching on the lakes, together with suitable imitations of other trout food, such as snails, shrimps, waterboatmen, various larvae etc. The six months of the season then left — April to (and including) September — offer a wide variety of food to the trout. And they offer the inevitable ups and downs of seasonal change to the angler.

A brief look at how each month fishes would go like this:

April
Main flies hatching are the chironomids or duck fly, and the lake olives. Fishing is mostly wet-fly, with pupae and nymph patterns most successful. Best in forenoon and early afternoon.

May
High-point of the year for many anglers. Main flies hatching are the mayfly (a decreasing species); the chironomids and olives, as in April; the claret dun; pale wateries; and caenis, or fisherman's curse. Best times for angling are the forenoon, afternoon and evening — all day really.

June
Much the same flies hatch in June as in May, except that the mayfly dies off around the middle of the month and the sedges begin to hatch. The most important sedges are the big red sedges, including the peters and murroughs, and the caperer, and the various types of silverhorns. In the latter half of the month, fish may not touch fly at all during the day, being "on the fry" — that is, eating the perch fry which are then at their most vulnerable. Fishing is best in the evening if sedges are about.

July
Almost as bad as late June but saved by the sedges. There are also chironomids and olives and a few land-bred insects may be on the water, including ants, black gnats etc. The Daddylonglegs is beginning to move and there will be damoiselle flies as well. Best time to fish is the evening rise to the sedges.

August
Surprisingly enough, often a good month. Chironomids and some lake olives, plenty of sedges. Often splendid fishing to the dapped Daddylonglegs or dry natural. If no dapping available, the evening sedges offer the best chances.

September
Sometimes the best month of all. Fish beginning to feed more eagerly as spawning time nears and early autumn rains bring fresh water. Daytime fishing is again back after an absence of a couple of months

but can be sporadic and uncertain. Evening fishing to sedges probably best but there will be lake olives, chironomids, the usual land insects and others.

So the fisherman's year, if in truncated form. I have tried to simplify it as much as possible, perhaps too much. But then not all anglers want to know much about the entomological names or habits of the flies on which the trout feeds. For those who do — and I promise the doubtful that even a slight entomological knowledge increases both pleasure and catches — the following table is supplied.

APRIL

Natural fly	Matching Artificial	Usual angling method	Best time to fish	Where best to fish	Useful comments
Chironomids Duck-fly (*chironomus* spp.)	Black & Blue	Wet	Forenoon and mid-afternoon for all	Shallows best	Widely present
	Black Pennell	Wet			
	Orange pupa	Wet			
	Olive pupa	Wet			
Olives Lake Olive (*cloeon simile*)	Green Olive	Wet	Forenoon and mid-afternoon	Usually shallows and bays	Dry fly often highly effective
	Sooty Olive	Wet			
	Olive Nymph	Wet			
	Pheasant Tail nymph	Wet			
	Ginger Quill	Dry			
Shrimp (*gammarus*)	Shrimp	Wet		Close to bottom	Fish very slowly
Water louse (*asellus*)	March Brown	Wet	Day time	Deeps	Major and neglected item in diet
	Brown Nymph	Wet	Day time	Deeps	

MAY

Natural fly	Matching Artificial	Usual angling method	Best time to fish	Where best to fish	Useful comments
Mayfly (ephemera danica)	Mosely May	Dry and wet	Daytime	Shallows	End of May
Spent Gnat	Spent Gnat	Surface	Evening	Near shores	May-June
Chironomids (chironomus spp.)	As in April plus Woodcock and Yellow	As in April	As in April plus evening	As in April	Pupa very good
Lake Olive (cloeon simile)	As in April plus Golden Olive	As in April	All day, evening fall of spinners	Shallows and near shores	Dry fly in calms
Pale Watery (centroptilum luteolum)	Pale Watery Little Sky-Blue Dun	Dry and spent	Evening Evening	Shorelines, calm bays	Spent patterns often effective
Claret Dun (leptophebia vespertina)	Claret & Mallard Claret Nymph	All Wet	All day All day	Peaty areas Peaty areas	Best in boggy lakes
Sedges Great Red Sedge (phryganea grandis and p. striata)	Murrough	Dry and spent	Evening	near shores, islands etc.	End of May. Hatch in deeps, swim to shore
Green Peter	Green Peter Green Nymph	All Wet	Evening Evening	As above As above	As above
Dark Peter	Green Peter	All	Evening	As above	As above
Black (Dark) Caperer (sericostoma personatum)	Halford's Welshman's Button	All	Daytime	As above	One of few day-flying lake sedges
Silverhorns (mystacides spp. and leptocerus spp.)	Brown SH Silver Sedge Invicta Wickham's Fancy	Dry and spent Wet	Evening	Wherever hatch is	Females fly out to lay in open water
Caenis	Pale Watery Last Hope	Dry Dry	Dawn and dusk Dawn and dusk	Hatch or fall of spinners	Go home
Lesser Waterboatman	Corixa	Wet	All day	Near reeds, weedbeds etc.	Fish mid-surface
Snail	Black and Peacock Snail pattern	Wet Wet	All day All day	Near reeds, weedbeds, rushes etc.	Fish slowly just under surface

JUNE

Natural fly	Matching Artificial	Usual angling method	Best time to fish	Where best to fish	Useful comments
Mayfly	As in May	As in May	As in May	As in May	First ten days only
Spent Gnat	As in May	As in May	As in May	As in May	
Chironomids					
Olive Midge	Olive Duckfly	Dry	Late	Shallows	Hatch over marl or
Green Midge	Hackled Green	Dry	evening		mud bottom; form
(Also known as	Midge				clumps
Buzzers)	Midge pupa	Wet			
Sedges					
As in May	As in May	As in May	As in May	As in May	As in May
Cinnamon Sedge	Cinnamon Sedge	Dry and spent	Darkness	Near shores	Deadly in right conditions
Black Gnat	Black Gnat	Dry	Daytime	Near shores	As in May
Lake Olives	As in May	As in May	As in May	As in May	As in May
Also					
Caenis,					
shrimp,					
corixa,					
waterlouse,					
snail					

July and August

Chironomids and sedges as in June; shrimp, snail, waterlouse, corixa, caenis, cranefly (daddy-longlegs), ants, black gnats; grasshoppers and damoiselle flies may also be blown onto water and may be fished either on the dap or with suitable artificials.

September

Medium-sized chironomids, lake olives, smaller sedges mostly, plus shrimp, snail, waterlouse, corixa and some caenis. Daytime fishing uneven and requiring settled weather. Evening fishing still best. Land-bred insects may be blown on water.

Chapter Three

Lake Angling Tactics, Daytime

The problems of decision — tackle and equipment — some preferences — daytime tactics — boat-fishing — a rich diet — the black gnat — the dry-fly — dapping — a day on Corrib

---

> *Sometimes too early, sometimes too late,*
> *Sometimes too small, sometimes in spate,*
> *Sometimes too windy, sometimes too calm,*
> *Sometimes too frosty, sometimes too warm,*
> *Sometimes too dirty, sometimes too clear,*
> *There's aye something wanting, when I'm fishing here.*

> G. P. Buddy

DAYTIME angling for lake trout in Ireland is best during the spring and very early summer, and the early autumn. In between and at the front end of the season, it is firstly indifferent and secondly, for the hardy.

That is not to say that trout may not be caught during the so-called bad times. Of course they can. Early spring, if you can stick the wind and cold, is a splendid time to catch fish whose condition however, is not always prime.

Irish lake anglers are as a bunch, stereotyped and unimaginative. Most have little entomological knowledge and seem determined to continue like that. Many fish one method only — wetfly — possibly using the same cast of three flies from one end of the season to the other. They catch fish of course; but I think they miss a great deal of educative fun.

They show drawbacks in other ways too. They have little knowledge of the way in which a trout lives or how the trout's food lives either. Many cannot name more than a half-dozen artificials — and don't wish to do more anyway. Altogether a dull lot.

If these words seem harsh, they are nonetheless true — as a generalisation, that is. Irish lake anglers may well be the way they are because they spend little enough time on the lake and when they are fishing, are unwilling to experiment and thus possibly waste valuable fishing time. But it is true to say that only in the last decade has the dry-fly begun to come into its own in the armoury of the lake angler in Ireland; and deep-nymphing and lure tactics are still relatively limited to the inquiring angler only.

I suspect that much of the traditional reluctance of Irish lake anglers to change may be due to the embarrassment of waters available. The British stillwater angler of reservoir, small lake and gravel pit knows what to expect — the stockie nine times out of ten, largely predictable in its habits, often a rainbow and because most British trout fisheries are much smaller than the major Irish lakes, their anglers usually have a fair idea of where the trout are to be caught.

For the Irish lake angler things are different. He arrives at say, the shores of Corrib with 68 square miles in which to fish. Often how and where he fishes is dictated by a boatman or ghillie determined to down oars at six o'clock on the dot and hasten home to his tea. The big Irish lakes are not mere lakes — they are inland seas, often hostile and dangerous but above all difficult to read and fathom comprehensively.

The patterns and methods of daytime lake fishing in Ireland have been dictated by these big lakes — long drifts often of over 2 miles and occupying an entire morning, inevitably covering much dead water; no drogues, no anchors, just a monotonous and mournful drift with the wind dictating the pace. Looked at like that, is it not a thoughtless way to fish?

Equipment

Rod — for wet-fly, over 10 feet. Glass is perfectly adequate. Cane is heavy and the best are the carbons or borons. A rod of less than 10 feet does not work a team of wet-flies as well as a longer rod, particularly the bob-fly.

Dry-fly — For dry-fly work, rods should be at least 9 feet long. A No. 6 line is about right but you can use lighter if you wish. Leaders should be at least 9 feet to 15 feet, except when fishing the sedge late at night when it is safe to come down to 6 feet or even less.

Reel — need not be an expensive model. Should hold the fly-line and

100 yards of strong backing and should not be too heavy or too light to balance the proper working of the rod. Anglers will know by the feel of their outfit whether this balance is being achieved.

Line — must weight-match the rod — that is, a Number 8 line should be used with a rod designed to take that weight. For wet-fly I prefer a No. 7 or even a No. 6. Line can be intermediate sinking, such as a wetcel II; slow sinking or quick-sinking; or sink-tip. Like an increasing number of anglers, I use a floating line for most of my wet-fly fishing.

Leader (or cast) — on average, 9 to 10 feet, with two droppers, although mine is often 12 feet or more. I like between two and three feet between tail fly and middle dropper and about the same between middle and top droppers. But I vary them. Droppers should stand out from the leader and should be at least 3-4 inches long.

Net — round and with a diameter of at least 16 inches and preferably 18. Fixed handle at least 36 inches long. A stone or piece of lead tied to the bottom of the mesh helps the net to straighten in the water.

Drogue — an old plastic bucket (don't use the baler in case you lose it) and a fifty-foot length of strong but light nylon rope will do.

Folding anchor — a great invention. They are small and fold up compactly and can be bought in any reasonable yacht chandlery. Get another length of 50-foot rope to hold it.

Cushion — essential to avoid sore bottom. Should allow water to run off and not soak in. I use a thick slab of polystyrene insulation stapled into a plastic sack. It floats if lost overboard, keeps out the wet and gives an illusion of warmth to the *derriere*. Tie it to the seats with string to stop it blowing away.

Knee-boots — definitely NOT waders — ordinary wellington boots will do. Do not wear anything leather, which gets slippy when wet and is noisy in a boat.

Waterproof trousers — absolutely a must if you wish to stay as dry as you can. Welded plastic material is fine, but they should be of good quality and not rip easily.

Jacket — waxed, the best you can buy, with a hood, storm cuffs and no leaking areas. A long one is best but the standard length — just about wader-top — will do.

Ball of string — has endless uses but best for tying oars to rowlocks, which you should always do, except when the boat has tholepins, which are much better in every sense.

Knife — none of your finicky little blades but a good strong knife. When you want one in a boat, you often want it badly. Keep it sharp and handy to you.

Scissors — always useful. I have an extendable scissors holder clipped to my jacket which retracts the scissors neatly when you've finished using it, thus keeping it out of the way. Scissors are made today with blunt ends so that they don't stab you in the chest and can remove hooks from a trout's mouth as well as cutting line, nylon, etc. without slipping.

Priest — many anglers kill their fish by knocking their heads on the boat, which is not alone tricky to do but also alarms every fish within 100 yards. A proper, lead-weighted priest or even a short, stout stick will do better.

Spare oar — it's easy to break an oar. I rarely act on my own principle here, since most hired-out boats have only one set of oars. Bring a spare if you can.

Baler — make sure there's one in the boat. If you lose it, use your hat, which brings me to . . . .

Hat — if you must wear one, make sure it fits tightly and doesn't blow off at the crucial moment when you're trying to land a good trout. Tweed is best — it's warm and is near-impervious to all but the heaviest rain.

Food and Drink — on the bigger lakes such as Mask and Corrib, always take plenty. You might well be marooned on an island for a day or so if you hit bad weather.

Matches or lighter — to light fires if marooned.

If this list seems unnecessarily long and bulky, every item's right to be with me when I fish is there because experience says it should be so. You can, of course, fish perfectly adequately without much of it. I prefer to be safe, warm and well-prepared (and above all, dry).

Other tips
Every angler has preferences and fixed habits. Here are some of mine.

1. Before starting fishing, usually the evening before, I arrange in one box all the flies I'm likely to use when fishing — dry and wet etc. I keep this in my jacket pocket so that I don't have to reach into my bag and scuffle around looking for various boxes when I want to change a fly.

2. If you carry two rods in a boat — and you should, one for wet and one for dry — mount them both before embarking. It is difficult and dangerous even to set-up a rod while in the boat. Stow your spare rod along the thwart — never on the bottom of the boat where you are bound to step on it.

3. Don't stand up to cast or fight a fish It allows fish to see you easily and will alarm them, whereas they are rarely alarmed by a boat itself. It is also discourteous to your boat partner, since he inevitably is fishing a shorter line than yours and your longer line will frighten fish coming to his flies. It is also highly dangerous.

4. Assuming two of you are fishing, one at the bow, one at the stern, without a ghillie, keep the net on the floorboards under the centre seat. That way either of you can reach it when in a fish and it won't be in the way.

5. Carry a torch — invaluable when evening fishing, useful for finding the pier or harbour late at night or even signalling if you're marooned in heavy weather.

6. If fishing from the shore, beware. Limestone lakes frequently have heavy deposits of limey mud, often feet deep, looking deceptively firm on top but a deathtrap. I have had one very narrow escape from being drowned through stepping on this mud and sinking over my head. I was saved by a friend nearby. Had I been on my own, you would not be reading this.

7.   If fishing the big lakes, use nothing less than a 6 horsepower outboard engine — and tie it to the boat. Western lake boats are 18 feet long and heavily built for a very good reason — they need to be. To be caught on a rocky lake in a storm is frighteningly dangerous. Do not take chances.

8.   If caught in a storm, head for the nearest island and land in its lee — that is, on the sheltered side. Never land on the weather side. If your engine breaks down in a gale, keep the boat's head to wind by rowing enough to keep her straight, at the same time allowing her to drift backwards and downwind to an island. Don't let the boat go broadside if you can.

9.   Never fish a strange lake without inquiring locally about it. It may have rocks, reefs, dangerous areas and so on. The western lakes, particularly Mask and Conn, are very rocky, with many rocks just under the surface and with razor edges of sharp limestone which will split a boat open with ease.

And that's enough of that for the moment. If there is one clear message in all that, it is: come well prepared and be careful.

Daytime angling tactics

April, May, early June and September are primarily the times for fishing during daylight hours. There will be dapping with the daddy and the hopper during late July, August and even early September but those months are more for evening angling. There is of course also evening angling in May, June and September but practically none in April.

We have seen from the previous chapter what flies ought to be on the water in any given month, and also what other food should be available to the trout such as snails, corixae (waterboatmen), shrimps and waterlice. Any approach to lake angling must be based on the availability of these foods to the trout. Certain foods, such as shrimps, are active more at night, while snails and waterlice are about all day.

The main task of the angler arriving at his chosen lake first thing in the morning is to look at all the factors which might affect his angling. They form two broad categories:

1.   *Weather conditions* — where the wind is from, is it stable or changeable, cold, warm or intermediate; the temperature of air and water; the weather forecast and what the day is likely to do.

2. *Likely fly life* — the time of year, even the particular month, determines largely what fly will be on the water. With even a little knowledge of natural flies and their ways, the angler should know which flies to expect, where and when they are likely to hatch; and know the matching artificial for those flies.

Are these not simple points? Yet they are ignored by hundreds of anglers. Observed and acted upon, those two categories of points to watch will bring the angler at least halfway to catching fish.

Boat-fishing

To those who have not yet fished Irish lakes, it seems odd that so little fly-fishing is done from shores. There are two main reasons — one that the big lakes provide better fishing around the outlying shallows and islands than the shore, the other that on many smaller lakes, heavy reed growth and boggy ground make shore fishing difficult and sometimes impossible.

That said, shore fishing still is curiously neglected. I rarely do it myself. I enjoy being in a boat, am able to cover more water and more fish and can fish the shoreline better than someone who is ashore. And I suspect most lake anglers are the same.

The traditional angling technique from a boat on an Irish lake is the long drift, as uninterrupted as possible, often a mile long or even longer and thus covering at least some ground which is "dead". The boat is allowed to drift unchecked with the wind, without drogue to slow it or rowing to quicken it or to vary its direction to either side of a drift. A team of wet-flies is cast out before the angler, retrieved and cast again usually on a medium-sinking line. Deep-sinking lines and lures, dry-fly, drogue techniques, quartering upwind, anchoring over the more productive spots — all these are considered more or less beyond the pale by the majority of lake anglers, although this too is changing.

Traditional methods have their value. On the right day, with the right wind, at the right speed, the long drift has its merits. On the whole however, it is unsatisfactory. Worse than that, it is unthinking. And it can be very unproductive.

The weakness of the traditional method is that it limits severely your chances of catching trout. Even moving at a moderate pace, a drifting boat allows perhaps seven or eight seconds for the flies to be in the water, by which time, even with a medium-sinking line, they will be perhaps six or eight inches underwater. On faster drifts, they will often not do more than barely penetrate the surface. As the boat moves onto the flies cast ahead of it, and as the angler retrieves, he is effectively keeping the flies stationary, or perhaps moving them towards him by a few inches only. Thus he is not working his flies properly and they are covering a limited amount of water only.

If you must fish the traditional free drift, vary your casting and your line of drift etc. Trout flies are more effective worked across a wave rather than straight through it. If two anglers are fishing, they can agree with each other to cast alternately on either side of the boat and bring their flies across wind and wave before retrieving back. Thus they cover more water and work their flies better, particularly the bob. A long rod helps here, perhaps even up to 11 feet or so.

I slow the drifting boat in anything of a good wind by using an old bucket tied to the gunwale with fifty feet of thin rope. The bucket is thrown out to the windward side and as the boat drifts, fills and sinks several feet. As the bucket is pulled along by the boat, it holds back the rate of drift very effectively. In a strong wind, a bucket thus used will slow a boat by at least half. The only thing to watch is using it in shallow water of under three or four feet, when it often hits bottom; but shortening the rope will bring it to the surface or near it. And when you steer fish upwind to play them, you must avoid them running under or across the rope by playing them directly off the end of the boat rather than off the upwind side.

Any drift, however short, has its hotspots. On a little lake which I fish, there is a shallow towards the middle over which I always slow the boat, and often anchor rather than drift straight across it. Often I am rewarded with a fish. Spots like this, such as an area where there is a sudden and concentrated surface hatch of flies or perhaps where trout are clearly feeding on the ascending nymph, should be fished out thoroughly by anchoring the boat. An anchor is indispensable in a boat and the folding ones are a godsend to the boat-angler. Anchoring is permitted on most Irish waters, unlike Britain.

Anchoring also allows the use of lines of different weights and types to get at the fish. After all trout do not feed at the one water-level all the time. They can be on the bottom, mid-water, surface or points in between. The angler must find these out.

Another lake which I fish has one end in which there is very deep water. When I first fished the lake I had five trout in a day in this small area, fishing a Golden Olive wet. After that I rarely did anything at all, finding it curiously fishless. Then I anchored in some 30 feet of water and fished a No. 8 deep-sinking line with a leaded nymph, a technique which though laborious and frustratingly slow, boated four good fish. My companion, fishing a conventional medium-sink line with a team of wet flies, raised not one fish. Without anchoring, and without using deep-fishing techniques, our day would have been blank.

The reverse is also frequently true. Emboldened by this success, I tried the same technique on another day in the same spot. I caught nothing for an hour while my companion (the same) landed two and lost two using surface techniques. In the end I hooked a trout which took my leaded nymph as it hit the surface at the end of a cast. The moral is obvious.

Anglers must recognise that all lakes are different — and even that one lake has many different facets, moods and conditions. Hatches can be very localised. Above all, it must be recognised that lake trout get certainly nine-tenths of their food under the surface and most of that on the bottom.

To grasp the richness of trout feeding in Ireland, examine the shoreline of a limestone lake, say a couple of feet out from the shore. I did this one day on the White Lake in County Westmeath, a noted haunt of big brown and rainbow trout. It is also the country's finest nursery for crayfish, the young specimens of which are favourite feeding for rainbows. In roughly one square metre of water I collected 16 snails of different sorts, seven shrimp, two waterlice, four waterboatmen (corixae) and six nymphs, as well as 18 individual caddis cases — the home of the sedge larvae. Add in the crayfish, the minnow, the perch fry and you have an idea of how much food there is on the bottom of an Irish limestone lake. The wonder, indeed, is that the trout bothers to feed on surface food at all. Perhaps, as they say, he does it purely for a change of diet.

I use this apparent digression as an example to show that an awareness of the various foods available in a lake, where they are most abundant, and how to match technique and fly to whatever the trout are taking is a prerogative to catching fish. If they are surface feeding, it will without doubt be either to emerging or adult fly, floating nymph or pupae, or snail — some species of snail float and trout take them as they float out from the stems of reeds and rushes. If trout are feeding underwater, it can be to almost anything. Mid-water can be ascending nymphs, pupae, snails or corixae. Deep-water and bottom feeding is often nymphal, where the trout are grubbing the nymphs out of weed and from behind stones; shrimp; larvae; perch-fry in the shallows and minnows the same. Techniques and flies must match what you think the fish are doing and where they are doing it.

I have distilled and greatly simplified a complex theory in that last

paragraph. I could write much of the living habits of trout food —
and it repays even slight study. But the essence of it all is that the
angler must think to match the trout and his appetite. Doing just that
may well mean the unhindered long drift; equally it can mean
slowing the drift, altering the casting technique, anchoring — all
these things and more.

Although my wet-fly fishing in lakes is done mostly with a floating
line, I carry several spare reels. One has a deep-sinking line, another
a medium-sinker. I carry always a dry-fly rod mounted in the boat.
Although it is tiresome and time-wasting, it frequently pays to
change reels and line and try something different. Adaptability and
a thinking, fresh approach to get inside a trout's behaviour are key
elements in any success.

In most lakes, taken as a whole, shallows are more productive than
deeper water. By shallows I mean anything up to nine feet deep or so.
The shallow shallows — under two feet — will rarely produce fish
during daytime. Fish have no eyelids and don't like bright sun; they
seek deeper water to avoid glare and predators such as herons who
stalk the shore. It is therefore, hardly worth your while to fish the
really shallow water during daytime.

At the same time, the feeding of trout in shallows is largely
misunderstood. Because shallows allow more light and heat into
their waters, weeds grow more quickly and thickly — and so does the
trout food which lives in them. Perch-fry and minnows, as well as
crayfish, are found in shallows. But trout keep away from them
during the day for many reasons. Only in the evening, when the
heron has gone home with the daytime angler and the picnicker, do
the trout move in to the now-sunless shallows to feed. Then is the
time to fish — but more of that in another chapter.

I am the strongest of believers in fishing carefully most shorelines
— not necessarily shallows. There are deep shores as there are
shallow ones. Above all there are many shores on many Irish lakes,
big and small, which are heavily reeded and rushed. Reeds and
rushes are limitless sources of trout food; their roots shelter nymphs
and larvae; their stems are feeding grounds for snails. And
particularly they are breeding grounds for the land-bred black gnat.

The black gnat is a much-misunderstood fly. Many anglers
confuse them with reed smuts, forgetting that reed smuts are
confined to running water. The black gnat is a small, black fly which
breeds terrestrially and in enormous numbers, is blown out over
water, and often forms large clumps during mating. Two black gnats
mating on the water and in the air are familiar sights.

In proper conditions, a fall of black gnats — and it is a fall and not a hatch over water — is irresistible to the trout. A lake which I fish has one heavily-reeded shore which is a traditional breeding ground for the black gnat. In the warm summery conditions which foster their emergence, I invariably head straight for the corner which yields me so many fish.

One day I rowed straight over the lake and eased my way up along the shoreline close to the reeds. The fish were in a perfect frenzy, breaking the surface all over the place to gulp the plenitude before them. In four casts my companion and I landed four fish. Truly the black gnat is an angler's friend.

The black gnat — and I rate this little fellow, at least on those lakes where it is abundant, as important a natural fly as any — underlines the weakness of the stoutly-held heresy of many lake anglers that the lee shore (that is the shore onto which the wind is blowing) is the best place for trout in a wind. I don't deny that it is frequently a larder of those flies which hatch out in water and are swept by the wind onto the lee shore. But the windward shore, particularly in a wind of any strength, is a rich source of land-bred insects blown onto the water by the wind. Such insects include black gnats, daddy longlegs, occasional grasshoppers, ants and many more.

In a wind, the windward shore, if at all sheltered, will have a belt of calm water. It is in this belt, and in the ripple immediately beyond it, that the wind-blown flies will fall — and it is there that the trout patrol for the feast. If you are an expert dry-fly angler, a size 16 or 18 Black Gnat, fished dry, is called for. If you are a little unsure and fear that you may disturb more fish in calm water, try the dry-fly in the pin-ripple beyond the calm. Or a small black fly of almost any sort fished wet but with a floating line is almost equally effective where the surface is a little distorted by the wind. There is no doubt though, that trout rise best on that calm belt, simply because there are more flies there and it is easier for the trout to see them and eat them, particularly if they are mating.

The dry-fly

Using the dry-fly is frequently a question of preference. I love the dry-fly in lake fishing but find it more effective on smaller lakes, where I am convinced trout rise more readily to it than on the larger lakes.

Daytime use of the dry fly is however, limited. On the whole, fishing wet, or just about sub-surface, even during a heavy hatch of

say, lake olives is more effective than the dry. The dry comes into its
own only — or almost only — when the surface is completely calm
or with the merest ripple.

I have already written about black gnat fishing on a windward
shore — a striking example of how killing a dry-fly can be on a lake.
The gnat is not the only exception. There are a few others.

The daddylonglegs — land-bred, this gangling and clumsy enemy of the
farmer can be deadly fished dry. I call him my secret weapon. He has
rescued many a poor day when fished randomly on the dry. Fished
as a principal, he is invariably a failure but brought on as a substitute
in the last despairing minutes of injury time he can win the match. It
is said you should fish him with a little pull now and then to make a
wake; I find he works just as well left severely still. Do not over-oil
him but dry him with brisk false casts. A friend in need is the daddy.

The lake olive — on a late summer day in say, early September, and
when the water is flat and still, olives often hatch well. In such
conditions your only hope is to fish dry. I find a size 14 to 16 Ginger
Quill as good as any.

Sedges — the caperer, or Welshman's Button, is a day-flying sedge. In
calm conditions a dry imitation works well sometimes.

Mayfly — if you dislike dapping, a dry Mayfly fished at random is
often just as good as the natural. Any big and bushy imitation will
do, especially in a wind.

Finally, the dry fly is always worth trying, especially when little
success has attended other methods. It should always be a part of the
lake angler's armoury.

Dapping

Many anglers profess a weary dislike of dapping. I like it — once in
a while. There is a fascination in watching the purposeful, head-and-
tail rise of the big trout to a live daddy; and it does attract some very
big trout indeed, often the biggest of the year.

Irish lake anglers will know the tackle and method too well for me
to describe it; but as it is peculiar to Irish and Scottish waters I will
expand just a little. Rod of from 12 to 14 feet or even longer, carbon
preferably but otherwise glass; fly-reel with no fly line — just nylon
of say 8 or 10 lbs. BS, a few yards of floss, a yard of nylon and a good-
sized hook, say size 8 or 9.

Stab the daddy or two daddies through the thorax, or thickest part of the body and thread onto the hook. Let out line, drifting before the wind, until the wind catches the light floss, billowing it out before you, so that the daddy floats out with it. Now lower the rod so that the daddy skips or dibbles on the surface.

When a trout takes — and if you are watching you will be left in no doubt at all of this — lower the rod so that he has time to turn and head down deeper into the water before he swallows. Count to three or four quite slowly and then raise the rod firmly but smoothly. As with all fish of any size, work him upwind to fight and land him; or if you are using a drogue out to windward, fight him off the end of the boat.

Dapping is simplistic but effective. It has, despite Kingsmill Moore's dismissal of it as "a melancholy pursuit", a certain charm of its own. I believe it to be no more effective than a dry daddy fished at random. But undoubtedly it is a unique way of lake fishing which should be tried. Whether it is fly-fishing is however, debatable.

Dapping, I should add, is not confined to the daddy. You can dap with grasshoppers (known in the west as harrys) or with that odd gastronomic offering, a daddy and a hopper or even a daddy and two hoppers. Or even, heaven preserve us, two daddies and a hopper in the middle. Enough, enough.

I cannot resist however, a little tale of dapping. Once in Wales, I found a small lake alive with trout feeding on daddies drifting across its calm surface. The dry-fly (I had no daddy imitation) proved useless. I tied in a length of ordinary garden cane between the top and bottom sections of my unfortunate fly rod and despite its creaking protestations and alarming droopiness, dapped with the natural daddies which were easily trapped in the clumps of rushes. In an hour my wife and I landed 27 trout. One up for dapping.

So much for success. I have had my failures. Once, fishing the dap on my own on Corrib, I rose and hooked a truly enormous trout. I shall not say his size, except to say, on my honour, that he looked half as long as the boat. He went under the boat, once hooked, with one irresistible surge; I managed to pass my rod under the keel, whereupon he turned and tried again from upwind. I was not ready for this tactic; as he tore under the keel again, the tip of my rod jerked down and caught on the windward oar.

That is not the only time I smashed a rod-tip but it is one of those times which still cause me to grit my teeth and turn in my bed at night. It seems, and was, careless fishing; yet the power of that great fish was such that I was almost powerless. I have refought that battle many times since and know now how I would handle it. But would he do the same thing?

My best day on the dap was a dark and overcast one, with a full and steady wind from the north. It's a wind which suits very well the shallows to the west of Corrib's biggest island, Inchagoill, an island of solitude and with echoes of a people long past who built on it a little stone church which still stands silent in its peaceful glade. Beside it is a standing stone of uncertain antiquity, but certainly the oldest inscribed standing stone in Ireland. A place of magic.

Inchagoill's western shallows are wide and long. You can drift for well over a mile or more and never stir from the finest of fishing water. Every yard here can hold a fish. I relieved a few yards of their denizens on that day and remember chiefly their remarkable similarity — seven trout averaging a pound and five ounces, with the biggest just over a pound and a half. Seven fish raised, seven hooked, seven landed.

Inchagoill, oddly enough, saw also my best day's fishing on Corrib. A morning of restless and thunder-threatened calm, punctuated only by the capture of one small and reckless perch who flung himself upon my fly mercifully succeeded by a long and sleepy lunch under the tall trees of Inchagoill. We awoke, my favoured ghillie and I, to hear the tips of those trees sough and sing mournfully. In the mounting breeze, on the eastern side of the island, we boated seventeen fish in just over an hour and a half.

Allowing for casting, playing, landing and sorting out tangles and hooks caught in nets, we were in fish almost constantly. All the fish, bar two, took a Claret and Mallard with such confidence that we had both reached that elevated stage where nothing seemed impossible, where we might, if given time, clear the entire lake of trout. Seventeen wild fish in an afternoon! Could it happen again! I will arise and go again, the sooner the better, and go to Inchagoill.

Chapter Four

Evening Lake Angling

A time for heavy trout — Glore and Ennell — sedges — silverhorns
— my biggest trout — a long fight — and safely landed

Arm'd, cap-a-pie, with basket, bags, and rods,
The angler early to the river plods:
At night his looks the woeful truth announce —
The luggage half a ton — the fish an ounce.

G. P. R. Pulman

EVENING angling for lake trout in Ireland is confined largely to
the summer months, coming into its own in late May, at its
best in June, July and August and tapering off through the end
of August and early September.

Other than the Mayfly, evening offers the best chances of really
big trout. There is little mystery in this; the heavy hatches of sedges,
plump and tempting, are one of the few times when it is worth a big
trout's trouble to feed on the surface to the hatching fly.

Much the best of the evening fishing is once again on the limestone
lakes. The size of trout which rise to a good sedge hatch is sobering.
On Lough Glore in County Westmeath, an angler friend saw from a
distance one September evening what he took to be otters
gambolling in the water. When he came closer he saw they were trout
— of such shattering size that when he speaks of it his hands shake.
There were dozens running from three to eight or nine pounds,
tempted to the surface by a great hatch of sedges.

Kingsmill Moore, in *A Man May Fish* tells a similar story of
picnicking one summer evening on Lough Belvidere (now Lough
Ennell, near Mullingar in County Westmeath) and finding himself
in the middle of one such event. Sadly, due to inadequate tackle, he
landed nothing. But such sights are familiar enough to those who
bother to spend time on the midland limestone lakes in the late
evenings. At no other time of the year, or of the day, will you get such
monstrous fish to rise. Not even the heaviest mayfly hatch will bring

31

so many and so big up to the fly. If you want big Irish trout, the evening sedge fishing is by far the best way to catch them on a fly.

Sedges truly are the fisherman's friend. For one thing, pattern is not half so important as size. In late evening, if the big sedges are about, almost any large, fuzzy pattern will do. It is true that silverhorns can make the trout finicky and fussy about size, colour and pattern; equally there are times when trout take the hatching sedge right at the moment of emergence and ignore the winged insect. But by and large, sedge fishing relieves the angler of much of the trouble of choosing the right fly of the right size.

For practical purposes, the sedges which the angler has to consider are few enough. There are the two peters, green and dark; there is the great red sedge, known in Ireland as the murrough; and there are the various silverhorns. Many anglers would throw in the caperer; but that little fellow is a day-flying sedge.

Evening sedge fishing is based on the emergence of sedges in the evening. The peters and murroughs hatch in deep water out from shore and when hatched, swim towards the shore. Silverhorn females fly out over the water to lay in open water. The successful angler bases his tactics, therefore, on the habits of these flies.

Much of my fishing is done in the evenings and on limestone lakes. Little enough of all that I have read about evening fishing seems relevant to the situations which face me. I am convinced that lake trout in Ireland feed little on the ascending sedge pupa but take it instead in three major ways — when it is hatching and trapped at the surface, and thus helpless to move, when it is fully hatched and buzzing towards the shore from deeper water, or finally when the female returns to open water to lay her eggs.

If that is true — and such is my experience, gained from watching these performances countless times — then wet-fly methods seem somewhat pointless. Therefore I use a floating line at all times when sedge fishing. I fish the pupa drowned in the surface film, without dressing; and I fish the dry-fly in the normal way.

I am in two minds about oiling a dry sedge; if there is a ripple — and very often there is not as the wind drops on the earth's turn and the coming of the night — I oil the fly. But if there is none, and I am confronted with the difficult and exacting conditions of still water, I feel that the stain of oil which inevitably spreads from an oiled fly must put trout off. Dry the sedge with quick false-casting, shorter than the actual cast, and it is as good a way as any on a windless evening of keeping it dry and floating.

There are several problems to be solved with this sort of fishing. It is easy enough to discover whether the trout are feeding on peters or on silverhorns. It is even relatively simple to distinguish whether or not they are feeding on pupae or adult sedge. The main problem is to place yourself so that you are both in a position to cover rising trout and at the same time not frighten them. If you are fishing from the shore — and that can leave you frustrated and out of reach much of the time — you will not generally frighten trout but you may well not reach them to cover their rises.

A vital point — and usually a forgotten or neglected one — is the position of the sunset and/or the last light of day. In calm conditions, drifting towards the shore with the evening light behind you is, if you think about it, nonsensical. Evening light is low and casts long shadows, which reach out ahead of you, warning the trout as you drift towards them.

Clearly you must in calm conditions fish towards the light. If this means fishing outwards from the shore, so be it. You will cast no shadow over fish, other than those behind you which you should already have covered. And you will gain the priceless advantage of looking into the afterglow, enabling you to see your fly better and any rise made to it.

On dark evenings, there is usually a breeze and less light from the sunset. And there will be little or no shadow. In these conditions, you are safe to drift with the light behind you; and fishing with whatever breeze there is is easier than fishing into it.

The working of your fly is also important. Big sedges buzz and scuttle about, often making a quite noticeable wake. The accepted theory is that you drag your fly a little when fishing dry, to imitate the scuttling sedge. It does work. But so does the sedge left strictly alone, particularly in calm conditions. I find that the unmoving sedge attracts more rises in calm conditions. But I would not care to be dogmatic about it. There are evenings when it works the other way.

I am conscious that many fine angler-entomologists, including Dick Harris and John Goddard, feel that trout also take the ascending sedge pupa. I think the trout does — but I am convinced that he does not take it half so readily as he does the hatching pupa, the adult fly swimming to shore, or the female laying her eggs. Each angler to his angle.

It is, as I have said, a reasonably simple matter to tell one sedge species from another. It is not necessary I would think, to be able to tell male from female or even one species from a similarly-sized and coloured one. But you must need to know the emerging habits of sedges and when the trout feed on these. The big sedges such as peters and murroughs are primarily sedges which emerge in late evening when the light is going. Silverhorns — a much under-estimated species — emerge earlier, sometimes in late afternoon but more often around teatime, say between six and seven. It is the female of this species which flies out well onto the lake before laying her eggs — and it is at that stage that the trout strikes.

I am acutely aware of how much of what I write about silverhorns directly disagrees with the writings of many anglers. John Goddard says very positively indeed that silverhorn imitations "are of little use to the fly-fisher" and that the silverhorn is rarely found in trout autopsies. That may be so in some waters. On the small lakes which I fish in the Irish midlands, it is assuredly not so. Dick Harris, perhaps the greatest living Irish angler-entomologist and with a vast experience of limestone lakes, says the trout feed on the adults. That they do so avidly I have not the slightest doubt. The silverhorn with its exceptionally long antenna, is relatively easy to distinguish (though other sedges also have long antennae) and in the autopsies which I have done (a process of which I am by no means fond) silverhorns have been present in considerable numbers.

I will not go on and on about silverhorns, other than to say that on many Irish waters they are of great importance to the evening angler. I fish a pupa dressing of my own which is basically brown with a twist of silver; a regulation silver sedge dressing suffices for dry-fly. Dick Harris ties a very effective deer-hair pattern. Sizes are important; I would go no bigger than size 10 or 11 and I quite often fish a 14 or even a 16. Whether to move your fly or not depends on conditions, just as it does when fishing bigger sedges. And I have the same feelings on oiling as I have for other sedges.

Evening sedging has given me some great fish and fishing. My biggest trout, which as I write stands nobly mounted in a case on my study wall, as stately and plump as any Buck Mulligan, was taken in total darkness on a mid-September evening on a small limestone lake. A day of wild wind and rain had been succeeded by a like evening. As darkness came, my companion Morrough (most aptly-named) and I were fishless. Then the wind dropped with the coming of night and I took a poorly-conditioned rainbow of some two pounds. It seemed our one and only fish of a dreadful day.

We were fishing out a last drift towards a shoreline guarded by dense reed-beds when ahead of us in the blackness I heard a trout feeding. Several times, casting with mechanical care, did I put my Green Peter where I thought the sound came from. No rise could be seen — it was impossible to see the other end of the boat even. So I twitched the fly gently towards me.

On the third or fourth cast there came a resistance, slight, then immovable. I tightened, whereupon it became movable, sheering off to the left from where I sat in the bow. I knew the fish was big. The very power of her run (for it proved to be a hen) thrummed solidly up the line to my fingers — I play fish with the hand rather than the reel. I could not see where she ran; only by bending low and sighting against the faintest of afterglows could I tell from my bending rod where the fight was taking place.

Try as I might, I could not persuade her upwind. In front of us lay the reed-beds. I lived in mortal fear lest she would run herself deep into their comforting shelter and send my cast twanging back. In the stern Morrough coped with and cursed a tangled cast.

I was aware suddenly that the boat was moving, slowly but enough to send a ripple spreading from the bow. I could not see it but I heard clearly the water parting on the stem. The trout was pulling the boat along. How big was this fish?

By now the battle had fallen into a pattern. The fish cruised back and forth in front of the bow some ten or twelve yards away. I could not gain more line nor could she. Now and then she varied this procedure with a spurt — although her stately power could not fairly or with dignity be called such — straight ahead, pulling the boat with her. Such control as I had was minimal. I kept the line tight, gave her some when she wanted it, though with reluctance, and took it back when she wasn't looking.

Looking back on it all, I had throughout the battle a clear head. My fears were many but at least I could reason with them. I must not let her get her head into the reeds. I must play her tight. But my point was a bare three pounds and by this time my fly must be a sad sight indeed. Would it hold? Or — horror of horrors — would she straighten it?

I had reached that stage where I must see the fish.

"Morrough — shine the torch."

Cursing me, the fish, the night and his tangle, Morrough fumbled forward and the beam of his torch lit the water. The bottom sprang up as though looked at through the bottom of a glass. We were in no more than a foot of water and almost aground. Then there swam deliberately into the circle of bright light a great silvered shape, the eyes bright as diamonds. In the calm water and the torch's sharp light, I could see the slender hold of the fly. My heart failed me.

It must be now. Or not at all. I put side pressure on the fish and she moved reluctantly to the side of the boat. Morrough put the net

under her in the torchlight and lifted her great bulk inboard. As he
did so the net bent and the fly fell out. But she was landed. And my
old Hardy scale, as accurate as any computer, put her at six pounds
and eight ounces. My biggest then and still.

One last thought on evening fishing with the sedge. On some
evenings in mid-summer you will find cruising fish working a line
usually parallel with the shore and picking up as they patrol all
manner of morsels — spent fly, emerging sedge pupae, adult flies and
so on. Fishing for them makes matters most trying for your heart.

The timing of the cast is vital. You must determine the line of
patrol and get ahead and well outside it. Then place your fly where
you think the trout will swim. Do not — above all do not — get
excited and flog the water to reach him. In calm conditions he will
sight the fly if it is anywhere on his path. Do not twitch it or move it
unless you are imitating a moving fly. Any movement unaccustomed
to his instinct will put him off. And when he takes — and oh, that
unbearable moment! — give him time to get his head down.

I have had some splendid fish in this way. It is a wonderful game
of catch-as-catch-can when you must outwit the trout. I once spent
an hour chasing and ambushing a large trout in this way before
laying the fly a foot from his nose as he travelled determinedly
forward. That was a noble battle in fading light — and a noble fish
of nearly five pounds. But you will not get many this way; I think
indeed that Irish lake trout cruise less than their English cousins.

The other prime time for evening fishing is the butt-end of the
mayfly season, when the spent fly or spent gnat, is on the evening
water. This is surface fishing, or sub-surface with the drowned
insect. It brings up mighty trout and demands techniques and tackle
identical almost to sedge fishing. It also, alas, brings on many more
anglers than would otherwise be found in evening fishing; and for
that reason I am not devoted to its pursuit.

Fishing from the shore is again chancy. Many Irish lakes are reed-
fringed and have boggy shores; they are both difficult and dangerous
to fish from. I feel fretful when fishing from a shore, always imbued
with the feeling that I am missing something and bereft of the means
to reach far-off fish. But every man to his taste. On the whole, Irish
lakes lend themselves significantly less to shore-fishing techniques
but it is nearly always possible to take a fish or two around islands
and shores in calm conditions where access is suitable.

Finally, it is the thoughtful approach by the angler to lake fishing
in the evening which will pay off — the approach, that is, of an angler
who *thinks*.

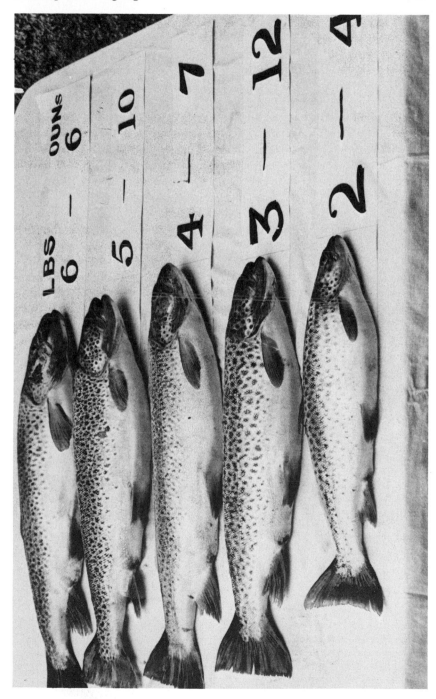

All aspects of angling change all of the time — some slightly, others more definitely. The countless factors inherent in all angling move and mingle and are never still. The successful anglers are those who watch for and notice the signs that these changes are taking place and who adapt their methods to suit the new pattern. Thus there is always room for experiment.

One form of experiment which is taking place is night fishing for trout on big lakes — and by night I mean after midnight. It is a lonely and often unnerving business being out on a big lake at night in a boat; in your imagination the rocks are clawing stealthily towards the keel, no friendly and reassuring lights twinkle out from farming homesteads along the shore; even the whine of the wind sings of unspeakable evils out in the dense darkness . . . .

But there is no doubt, no doubt at all, that on such nights big fish are on the move. And on such nights it is often the only time of the year, other than during the mayfly and a night or two on the big sedges, that the great trout which are in every big lake can be caught.

The techniques for this fishing are at a formative stage in Ireland. A calm night is essential if you are to hear and thus locate feeding fish. Dry-fly or surface fishing (where the trout can more easily locate the fly seen from below and silhouetted against such faint light as there is) is the likely method. One angler has captured a series of fish between four and six pounds using a buzzer and fishing until two or three o'clock in the morning. He is not the only one to say that on the lake which he fishes, night-time is the only time during which the biggest fish move and take fly.

Night fishing for big trout may well emerge as *the* significant way in which they can be caught. But it is essentially angling for the dedicated, even for the hunter of big fish. Not many are brave enough, determined enough, interested enough — even, perhaps, foolish enough? — to do it. But it is certain that it is a time when the big trout, for a time at least, lose some of their caution.

(PREVIOUS PAGE)
Five wild brown trout weighing a total of 22 pounds and 11 ounces, taken in Lough Sheelin in County Cavan in the days when this superb lake was unpolluted by phosphorus from pig-slurry. Noted for big fish, Sheelin produced many like these five — all of which were caught on Connemara Black, Green Olive and Sooty Olive, three unique Irish tyings.

Typical trout from Ireland's limestone rivers, where the high alkalinity and clear water produce heavy weed growth and excellent breeding conditions for invertebrate life.

SECTION TWO

Brown Trout in Rivers

(OPPOSITE)
An all-too familiar sight on many Irish rivers today; the River Funcheon in County Cork, an excellent tributary to the Blackwater, has been a consistent sufferer from wanton pollution. Here local anglers remove hundreds of dead trout from the river.

Chapter Five

The River Trout

An uphill battle — declining rivers — Barrow and Suir — the Boyne
drainage — types of water — limestone streams — other rivers

> *The waters fall and flow,*
> *By fragrant bank and still below,*
> *The great three-pounders rise and take*
> *The Palmer, Alder, Dun, or Drake.*
> *Now by the stream, if there you be,*
> *I prithee keep a place for me.*

John Buchan

IRELAND is so singularly well-endowed with good fishing rivers
that it would seem difficult in the extreme to reduce the quality
of its river trout angling to the extent that it has been reduced. Yet
that is the case. Today river angling is in the most desperate state.

The reasons are many and obvious. Pollution and over-fishing,
allied to poaching, lack of care, inadequate re-stocking and a general
couldn't-care-less attitude not alone by the public but almost
unbelievably by anglers themselves are prime causes. Add to this an
insensitive and arrogant official attitude to the difficult question of
arterial drainage and the picture is most bleak.

That fish not alone manage to breed in the midst of this holocaust
is surprise enough. That some rivers even manage to produce
reasonable angling is an even greater surprise. The richness and
vigour of the feeding on Irish rivers, most of all in its very
considerable body of limestone waters, manage partially to
overcome the depredations done on them.

We Irish are gradually if slowly being educated into a more
responsible attitude towards the environment generally, an attitude
which has, to be fair, extended to conserving the country's waters.
But it is a slow and wearisome process, bedevilled at every turning by
setbacks of every conceivable sort and monstrosity. Until it quickens
and becomes general, Irish rivers will continue to deteriorate.

Scientific surveys, which there is little space to enlarge upon here, confirm the trend towards total pollution; and while the picture in terms of European comparison seems healthy enough, a similar picture of comparison with our rivers of say twenty or thirty years ago is sobering.

I make an occasional habit of returning now and then to fish some of the rivers and streams which so delighted me in my childhood. I remember, for instance, superb trout fishing on the Barrow near Borris in County Carlow, an incomparable river in its prime; I have still a photograph of three brace of truly splendid trout whose rubicund shape belied their fighting qualities. They were caught under one of the many decaying weirs which are scattered along this noble river — a slanting and curving rim broken into little pools and run by trees and shrubs, and along whose length an entire day could be spent in search of the trout below. But a recent visit brought severe disillusion; today the Barrow struggles to efface the constant streams of effluent of all nauseous types which enter it seemingly freely at almost every turn. I shall not go there again.

And the Suir! How my angler's heart bleeds for that prince of trout rivers, whose dry fly fishing Lord Grey of Fallodon thought to be even better than his own beloved chalk streams of Hampshire.

I recall a July evening on one small and quiet run beneath a fast stickle landing three trout in four casts, like peas from a pod, weighing in total nearly eight pounds and all caught on a Sherry Spinner of venerable age and decrepit apparel. The Suir today, although it looks as lovely in its meandering green valleys beneath the swooping hills, is enough to make one weep. Pollution has dipped its fingers here too with an insistent unstoppability.

Some of the streams — they are hardly rivers — which I fish are small streams of the limestone plains. Not alone are they polluted and becoming more so; they have been through that process of "improvement" known as drainage, as iniquitous and apparently incurable as only bureaucratic obstinacy and arrogance can render it.

Here a decade or so ago, were prime limestone waters, wandering placidly through their levelled tableland of deep meadow, alder-fringed, with banks of yellow iris and wild mint their characteristic companions. Now they are drains, straight and levelled, without pool and run; their banks are high — often 20 feet and more and so steep that no angler save a goat can tackle them.

Drainage indeed; these rivers today resemble nothing so much as a drain. They have been gutted so as to provide quick run-off for heavy rain, to prevent flooding and to free hitherto winter-inundated land for round-the-year usage by farmers; but in summer so quick is the run-off that often they are left almost without water, pathetic trickles of weed-grown rivulets supporting little.

Nothing apparently can sway the official policy that this state of affairs is desirable. No angler would argue against the farmer's right to have his land freed of flooding; but there are other ways of doing it, ways which take some note of what the angler — and the conservationist — wants.

Weep — yes I could, and a thousand others with me!

The miracle of those "drained" streams is that they do recover. The Boyne system, which saw the drainers at their very worst, has crept back. The trout are there, if slowly; and if left alone and safe from the periodic cleaning operations which are threatened, they will be there in numbers.

It is astonishing and comforting to see how nature beats even man in her patient overcoming of his worst excesses; a tree falls in and lodges. Silt collects and debris with it. Suddenly there is a run and a pool. Stones topple down the banks and the thirsty cattle tread the loose gravel into the bottom. There is a stickle, below it another fast run. Weeds thrive in the rich, limey water and now there are solid beds, around which the water loops and gushes. And if you are in the river wading, and your eyes unconscious of the horridness of the mutilated banks, you are aware of the water's own character again.

It would not be pushing matters too far to say that Ireland's rivers and streams are still fishable and producing fish simply because of nature's marvellous regenerative powers. This is not to ignore the work of the former Inland Fisheries Trust, now the Central Fisheries Board; but the work of that worthy body has inclined more to the development of lake rather than river angling. Rivers and streams by their very nature are more vulnerable in many ways than are larger bodies of still water; and the widespread habit of the Irish of dumping even household refuse into running water in the blinkered expectation of it being washed away to some mythical and all-embracing cesspool seems frustratingly irreversible.

To cloud further this dismal scene, the country's trout angling clubs are almost anonymous. It is difficult for outsiders to understand why this is so. English anglers in particular, accustomed to patrolled and keepered trout streams, find the approach to looking after Irish rivers incomprehensibly loose.

But figure it this way; a local club with say ten miles of river in its "control" will have perhaps thirty to fifty members, of whom rarely

more than half a dozen are fishing at any given time. The remainder
of the angling population, both inside and outside the club's area, see
no reason at all why they should not angle in a river which they see
as much their property as anyone else's. So the club angler, who has
paid his fee, will often find himself crowded off from his fishing by
anglers who pay no attention whatsoever to their illegal status.

Enforcement of laws in angling is a widespread joke in Ireland;
and the essential anarchic character of the rural Irishman, together
with his loose interpretation of the law, means that the control of
angling is perilously fragile.

There is more, much more, that is wrong with Irish angling in
trout streams but I will go no further along this sombre road. Suffice
to say that anglers from other countries, tempted by tales of
wonderful trout fishing in these streams, may well find those
promises hollow. Any angler arriving in Ireland who has not made
careful plans beforehand and who expects good trout fishing will
quite simply not get it.

For all that, there is still plenty of trout angling of reasonable
quality in Irish streams and rivers. I was brought up on river angling
and it remains still my first choice. Although my field of angling in
running waters has shrunk, I still have a central core of half a dozen
rivers where I usually have some excellent fishing, given the ups and
downs of weather and other conditions. These streams have yielded
me an average 150 takeable trout for each of the past five seasons —
not that I have killed more than a dozen of those trout.

With my fishing outside of holidays confined to evening and
weekends, I averaged three good trout an outing — and that on
rivers where another angler is a comparative rarity once June is past
and the weeds take over.

I know that throughout Ireland are many anglers with similar
local knowledge — a knowledge which wisely they keep to
themselves. We have all, when less wise, divulged the whereabouts
of our favourite fishing spots, only to arrive the next time and find a
dozen anglers flogging our secret water with artificial minnows,
worms and the like. I once found a splendid stretch on an eastern
river where literally no other angler trod — the river had been
drained and unknown to anyone, the trout had come back. One
evening I took three trout in quick succession weighing together a
little over four and a half pounds; and so elated was I that I disclosed
this information to a fellow-clubman. That was that. A week later I
found five anglers on "my" stretch; and so disgusted was I that I
have stayed away since.

This defensive selfishness, possibly less familiar in the more ordered rivers and streams of Britain, is necessary in Ireland. What you have you keep to yourself. Do not therefore, if you are a visiting angler, expect to be clasped to the friendly bosom of the local angler. He will wish you no ill other than to go as far away as possible with the greatest haste and least knowledge.

Types of water

Broadly speaking, there are three main types of river and stream in Ireland. They are (a) limestone waters; (b) non-limestone waters and (c) upland streams.

Limestone waters are the nearest Irish equivalent to the chalk streams of England. I have been fortunate enough to fish the Test and Driffield Beck, two of Britain's finest chalk streams; and while the clarity not so much of the water as of the stream bed is markedly different, on the whole Ireland's limestone streams support much of the same sort of animal and plant life as do the chalk streams.

The major difference lies in the fact that British chalk streams are fed mostly by springs of pure water which has been filtered to a brilliant clarity through the chalk beds near the rivers' sources. Thus they are less susceptible to rain and on the whole run clear and full for most of the season. Irish rivers are mostly rain-fed; and while limestone, which is highly porous, fills a similar role to chalk, it is a dark stone and forms an opaque bottom above which it is often very hard indeed to see a trout. Thus the situation on most British chalk streams, where the angler can often spot and watch his trout feeding over clear yellow or white gravel, hardly ever occurs in Ireland. Fortunate indeed is the Irish stream angler who can watch his quarry underwater.

Other than that however, Irish limestone streams are markedly similar to the great chalk rivers. They produce exceptional trout — fat chunky fellows whose average weight might not perhaps match exactly those of their British cousins but who are more often of wild stock than of farm origin. The feeding on these limestone streams, beside the classic upwinged ephemeroptera, is immensely rich — this great limestone table groans with shrimp, crayfish, snails, waterlice, corixae and a thousand other delicacies.

Foreign anglers used to the fly-life on Test or Kennet will find familiar friends cocking a wing as they drift over the trout. Here are the large dark olives of early spring, the iron blues, the mayflies, the blue-winged olives and the sedges. There are some flies absent from Ireland such as the grannom; but on the whole, the selection of natural flies is not markedly different.

The limestone streams of Ireland are widespread — limestone is one of the bases on which the country stands. The central plain, which is mostly base limestone, spreads searching fingers into the counties which adjoin it, such as Tipperary, Clare, Limerick and Galway. Curiously, the central plain's major river, the Shannon, is not a good trout fishery, although it does hold huge trout; and some of the area's biggest rivers, such as the Suck, are better as coarse fisheries.

Probably the best limestone river has been the Suir in Tipperary, though pollution has changed that. But typical limestone waters are the Little Brosna, particularly in County Offaly; the Maigue in County Limerick; the Fergus in County Clare; the Black River in County Galway; the Boyne in County Meath. This is a very abbreviated list; but almost any river or stream touching on the central plain of limestone can be classed, if loosely, as a limestone stream.

The richness of the limestone streams brings with it truly staggering weed growth — the major problem facing the Irish stream angler after say, June. Most limestone streams where weed is not cut — and this is the majority — are barely fishable after early summer, especially with wet-fly. Even the skilled dry-fly angler may find himself faced with tiny runs between weeds or small pools and open stretches hedged threateningly with massive beds. This makes for exciting but demanding fishing.

Thus the spring of April and May are the best and easiest times to fish the limestone waters. There is usually plenty of water and not enough weed to trouble the angler. After that he will find himself gradually pushed into evening fishing. Which is no bad thing in itself.

On these limestone streams and rivers, you may expect trout of a good average — between ¾ and 1 lb. is usual. There are plenty of bigger trout but it takes something to make them rise — a good hatch of blue-winged olives or sedges will sometimes do it.

It is significant too, that you will find these big trout in even the

OPPOSITE:
Well-hooked, this good limestone trout boils under the rod's pressure on the River Suir in County Tipperary. Typifying the pollution problems which face many Irish waters, the Suir was an incomparable dry-fly river in years past and considered by Lord Grey of Fallodon to be even better than the famous chalk streams the Test or Itchen. On its day still the best limestone river in the country, the Suir still has some fine fishing but faces an uncertain future.

smallest streams; I once, out of laziness, followed a tiny tributary of quite a small limestone stream, casting lackadaisically up its narrow length — it was no more than four feet wide — and hooked a stupendous trout of at least three pounds which having taken my fly before my startled eye, hung it and my leader round a trailing blackthorn branch and flounced off upriver leaving behind a wake which washed half-way up my waders. Since then I take care and caution in these tributaries and have had my reward of fish well over two pounds.

The second loose category of stream and river is the non-limestone one, which I unhesitatingly revise a little to include waters with some alkaline level but not enough to put them into the limestone category.

Many of these waters are either slightly alkaline or neutral. The feeding is much the same as that on the pure limestone waters but is not so good and so plentiful. These rivers too, offer more broken water than the slow streams of the central plain. Weed growth is not so heavy either and the wet-fly man can often fish throughout the season.

Rivers in this category would include the Slaney in Counties Wicklow and Wexford; the Blackwater in Cork and Waterford; the Nore in County Kilkenny and several other largish rivers, with many, many streams also falling into this classification.

The third category comprises all those small streams, mostly non-alkaline to acidic, which are for the most part confined to the hilly and mountainous areas. You will find these in coastal counties mostly, especially those counties which have mountain ranges — Donegal, Mayo, Galway, Kerry, Wicklow and several others.

They will often hold a prodigious head of small brown trout and if you are that way minded, it is nothing to catch forty or fifty on a good day. You will ,however, put them back — please; for these trout are of excellent size if they go anything lower than a half-dozen to the pound. You fish these for fun and not for fish.

If these streams have another positive use to the angler, it lies in their value as a training ground for youngsters. Wet fly downstream is easier for the beginner than dry fly upstream; and if the youngster can put his fly on the water at all, he will catch fish. To catch a fish for anyone starting angling is a wonderful boost to morale and determination to catch another one. And if the beginner can be taught to fish a fly without barbed hook, and to handle and release his fish gently and humanely, a good day's work will have been done both in the name of angling and of conservation.

Chapter Six

The River Season

The fishing season — a day on the Iron Blue — natural flies and matching artificials — the season by month — a short-list of patterns

---

Only an idle little stream
Whose amber waters softly gleam,
Where I may wade through woodland shade
And cast the fly, and loaf and dream.

Henry van Dyke

I N theory, the river trout angler can fish from mid-February to the end of September. In practice, few anglers start to fish seriously any earlier than St. Patrick's Day on March 17th, which for many of them traditionally marks their first true day on the river. For many more effective angling starts in late March-early April and ends when the weed growth threatens to clamber from the river and envelop the surrounding countryside in late June.

Late February and early March, if the winter has been mild (and most Irish winters tend more and more to be just that) sees the first real hatch of fly with the large dark olive *(baetis rhodani),* which hatches around mid-day. Sailing serenely down the current, he is a gladsome sight, both to trout and angler; and he brings with his coming the first sustained rise of the year. But you must be quick; this early in the season it is only the brief hour around mid-day which tempts both insect and trout. And by one o'clock or two o'clock you may go home.

Late April, which often brings with it sharp, gusty and cold weather, brings also my favourite river fly — the iron blue. This smallish, dark olive is passionately favoured by the trout; and he has given me some of my finest river fishing if not in actual bag size, then surely of enjoyment enjoyed. I still see, as though it were this morning that it had happened, a stretch of a small limestone water, a stretch no longer than eighty yards, at the top of which, beside a little bridge, the farmer who owned the land was constructing a cattle grid. The day was bitter and grey, with a gusting cross-stream wind bringing flurries of hail. But as I started up the stretch, the iron blues came onstream like some endless flotilla. So did the trout. In just under an hour I landed seven fish between three-quarters of a pound and a pound, two of which I kept.

When I reached the top of the stretch, I paused for a chat with the farmer. I gave his young son the two fish, went down to the beginning of the stretch and started up again. The hatch was strong as ever, as was the appetite of the trout. And fishing over the identical water, I caught exactly another seven fish, all of even weight, all of which I returned. Mid-way through this performance (which I may say I have never repeated) I glanced up to see both farmer and farmer's son gazing at me with awed respect etched visibly on their faces. If flawed elsewhere, surely my fishing prowess lies in secure reputation in that quarter at least.

Late May should see some mayfly — if there is any at all. It should see too, the tremulous first questing of the new season by the blue-winged olive, a major fly in the scheme of things.

Late May normally sees, on those rivers fortunate enough to harbour it, the arrival of the mayfly. And more importantly, since it is one of the most important summer flies on Irish rivers, the first of the blue-winged olives should be hatching, along with various olives.

June, which is really the peak of the angling season, with plenty of water and warm weather, has plentiful olives of all sorts and also sees the first heavy hatches of sedges, including the day-flying sedges such as the grey flag and the caperer or Welshman's button (which is also an evening hatcher). Black gnats can be important locally and the caenis makes its unwelcome appearance. Let us not too, forget the alder, which times its arrival roughly to that of the mayfly and which often gives superior fishing; although whether the fish take the artificial for the natural is doubtful.

July sees much the same flies as June, except the alder and mayfly. But day fishing has declined and only the blue-winged olive, pale evening dun and the various evening sedges give reliable evening dry-fly fishing.

August is much the same as July, but at the month-end can occasionally give good daytime fishing. September, with the evening shortening quickly, sees daytime fishing gradually get better and that of evening curtailed. It can be one of the best months.

The following table of emergence of natural flies by month needs more than a little qualification. It is possible but very wrong to be dogmatic about any aspect of angling and so it is with this table.

The height of an Irish mayfly hatch; despite pollution problems and the mysterious ups and downs of mayfly patterns of breeding, hatches remain generally good in Ireland on most of the major lakes, although it has disappeared from Sheelin and many of the major rivers.

What I have tried to do is to provide the roughest of guides to the type of fly which should, by nature, be hatching when and where, the most common patterns of artificial flies to match the natural, and a few hopefully helpful and enlarging hints.

I will qualify it further by pointing out the wide variances between types of rivers. Many rivers will have large gaps in the range of flies which hatch there. Flies in Galway do not hatch simultaneously with flies in Wicklow, nor those of Cork with those of Cavan. If you must follow my guide, do so with a loose interpretation and expect not to find enormous mayflies in great droves on some mountain trickle.

APRIL

Natural fly	Matching Artificial	Usual angling method	Best time to fish	Where best to fish	Useful comments
Olives Large dark olive *(baetis rhodani)*	Hackle Greenwell Gold-Ribbed Hare's Ear Rough Olive	Dry Wet and dry	Mid-day	Follow local hatches	Rough Olive best in slow water
Spinners	Lunn's Particular Red Spinner	Dry Wet	Afternoon and early evening	On or below faster stretches	Spinners best in warm weather
Olive *(baetis tenax)*	Light Olive	Dry	Mid-day	Localised hatches	*B. tenax* important late April
Dark olive *(baetis atrebatinus)*	Dark Olive	Dry	Mid-day	as above	
Iron blue *(baetis pumilus)*	Iron Blue	Dry	Mid-day and early afternoon	Localised hatches	Hatches best in cold weather
	Snipe and Purple March Brown	Wet Wet	As above All day	As above Faster rivers	As above Confined to eastern rivers
March brown *(rhitrogena haarupi)*					
Iron blue spinners	Little Claret Jenny Spinner Houghton Ruby	Dry Dry Dry	All day All day All day	Below faster stretches	Jenny Spinner is male. Female lays in fast water
Others Early stonefly *(protonemoura myeri)*	Orange Partridge	Wet	All day	In fast stretches	Will imitate several stoneflies
Shrimp *(gammarus pulex)*	Shrimp	Wet	Daytime and early evening	Near weeds on bottom	Fish deeply
Water louse *(asellus)*	March Brown	Wet	As above	As above	As above

MAY

Natural fly	Matching Artificial	Usual angling method	Best time to fish	Where best to fish	Useful comments
Olives; most of those as in April plus;					
Pale watery (centroptilum luteolum)	Sky-blue Dun Blue Quill	Dry Dry	Daytime	Follow hatch	In warm weather at dusk
Pale evening dun (procloeon rufulum)	Pale Watery	Dry	Evening	Slower stretches	Best in hot weather
Blue-winged olive (ephemerella ignita)	Blue-winged Olive Orange Quill BWO nymph	Dry Dry Wet	Afternoon and evening	At emergence	Late May
BWO spinner Mayfly (ephemera danica)	Sherry Spinner Mosely May Greydrake Spent Gnat	Dry Dry Dry Wet	Evening Daytime Daytime Evening	Where spinners fall At emergence	Spent patterns often best
Yellow evening dun (ephemerella notata)	Yellow Evening Dun	Dry, wet and nymph	Dusk	Quicker limestone rivers	Wet fly good in fast water
Yellow May dun (heptagenia sulphurea)	Yellow May	Dry	Daytime		Sparse hatch
Caenis (caenis spp.)	Tiny Pale Watery	Dry	Dawn and dusk	Slower stretches	Go home
Sedges					
Great red sedge (phryganea grandis and phryganea striata)	Murrough Red Sedge Sedge Pupa	Dry Dry Wet	Evening Evening Evening	Wherever they emerge	Any large bushy fly will do
Alder (sialis)	Alder	Dry	Daytime	At emergence	Land-bred — fall on water

MAY — continued

Natural fly	Matching Artificial	Usual angling method	Best time to fish	Where best to fish	Useful comments
Grey flag (*hydropsyche* spp.)	Grey Flag	Dry	Daytime	Quicker stretches	Spent good in evening
Black caperer (*sericostoma personatum*)	Welshman's Button	Dry	Daytime	At emergence	Small hatch
Hawthorn (*bibio marci*)	Hawthorn	Dry	Daytime		Falls on water
Black gnat (*b. johannis*)	Black Gnat	Dry	Daytime		Falls on water
Yellow sally (*isoperla*)	Yellow Sally	Dry and wet	Daytime	Stony stretches	
Reed smut (*simulium*)	Black Gnat	Wet	Daytime	Quicker water	Erroneously called Black Gnat
Others Snails, shrimp, corixae, waterlice					

Notes to table

Several species which may be important locally have been left out of this list, including the summer mayfly which is good on some of the Clare rivers. Again these lists are to be interpreted or followed loosely, as rivers vary as much as do their hatches. If the angler were to choose a short-list, those patterns without which I would not venture forth would include a Hackled Greenwell, Gold-Ribbed Hare's Ear, Pheasant Tail nymph, Black and Silver, Iron Blue Dun, Orange Quill, Coachman, Silver Sedge, Green Peter and assorted nymphs and pupae, not forgetting a daddylonglegs.

June
Olives — much the same picture as May, with the addition of the small dark olive *(baetis scambus)*, artificial patterns of which are best fished dry, both in the daytime and the evening. Blue-winged olive of increasing importance.

Sedges — much the same as May, except that the grey flag is absent largely. An important addition are the peters, both green and dark. Dry patterns are best, but do not neglect the pupa patterns. Best in the evenings on slower stretches below lake outfalls — the peters are primarily lake species.

Reed smuts — often confused with the true black gnat *(bibio johannis)* the reed smut can have an impact greatly belying his tiny size. They hatch mostly in faster water in the daytime. Tiny dry imitations best.

Others — land-bred insects may include ants. Some damoiselle flies. There are also black gnats and of course snails, shrimp, corixae and waterlice.

July
Blue-winged olives, pale wateries, pale evening duns are the most important olives. Sedges also important. Reed smut and caperer also to be considered. Evening fishing predominates.

August
Much the same as July. Look for land-bred insects etc. falling onto water, including daddylonglegs. Again evening fishing best.

September
Blue-winged olives, smaller sedges and pale wateries. Daytime fishing slowly resuming.

Chapter Seven

Daytime Angling Tactics

The early months — tackle and equipment — the wet-fly — upstream and downstream — wet patterns — a Nore expert — the dry-fly — invertebrate drift — caenis — nymphing

> *There are trout in my river whose attitude,*
> *Is one of the blackest ingratitude;*
> *Though I offer them duns,*
> *most superior ones,*
> *They maintain a persistent Black Gnatitude*

Anon.

EFFECTIVELY daytime angling for river trout excludes the months of high summer — July and August. As with all fishing statements, there are exceptions to this one. But the rule is a good rule-of-thumb one and will suffice for our purpose.

The early months, up to the end of June, are the high point for the wet-fly man. Thereafter weed growth, particularly on limestone waters, is his bugbear. In addition summer water levels can be low and currents slack, giving him little chance to work his method properly. Late June to September are those times when the dry-fly comes into its own.

To fish Irish rivers effectively throughout the season, the angler must be able to switch from wet to dry and to include as well the use of the nymph in his armoury. I do not confine myself to the dry only but I prefer it to the wet and find myself not a whit disadvantaged.

Many Irish rivers and streams would blanch the cheeks of an Englishman accustomed to manicured banks. Quite literally it is often difficult to put a fly on the water, let alone cover a rising fish. Few waters are cared-for to any extent so hard work is often the order of the day.

Tackle
Rods — I use an eight-foot Hardy Fibalite Perfection for dry-fly work

on small rivers and streams. I do not claim it to be better than anything else but it suits me, is accurate, tough and reliable, and holds a No. 6 line comfortably. Small rods for small rivers, slightly larger for bigger. Cane is best for wet-fly, about nine feet or so.

Reels — as light as possible. Use 50 yards of braided nylon backing.

Line — ignore a general tendency to weighty lines. Both dry and wet need go no heavier than 7. Carry both wet and dry lines on separate reels if you have room.

Leader — my dry-fly leaders are not less than nine feet and often 11 or even 12. I grade them downwards from line tip, to which I attach permanently with a needle knot about 15 inches of 16 lb. nylon. After that comes a length of 12 lb., then 8 lb., then 5-6 lb. and finally about two feet or more of a 3 lb. point, and even occasionally, of 1½ lb. I renew the point probably at least once a session. I find this graded leader turns over well and presents a cocked fly perfectly eight times out of ten. Anything less than a 3 lb. point will not keelhaul heavy trout in weeded water in high summer. Wet-fly leaders are dealt with later in this chapter.

Other items

Waders — preferably studded felt soles. Rubber slips on weedy rocks. Thigh waders are most useful.

Clothing — must be rain-proof and should not "sweat". Waxed cotton (Barbour, Maxproof etc.) are the best. Should be light model and cover wader-tops. And have a hood.

Bag — better than a basket. Buy a good one (Liddlesdale I find superb), with a removable fish pocket and two outside pockets.

Net — an unsolvable problem to manufacturers apparently. I made my own from a brass curtain rail and a cane from a chimney-cleaning set. The upper half of the handle unscrews, making a good wading net, and I use the loose handle as a priest when I need to kill fish. Weight the bottom of the mesh with a stone and hang high enough on your person to avoid it catching in weeds and bushes on the bank.

Fly-boxes — spend money on them. They should be of tough aluminium. I find Wheatley boxes the very best — you can sit on them, stamp on them and they remain solidly unaffected.

Scissors — buy one of those useful gadgets from which you hang the scissors and which you pin to your jacket. A spring allows you to pull the scissors out and then retracts it. There are excellent custom-designed scissors now on the market which have blunt ends, pliers-like tips and saw blades — very useful.

Knife — always carry one — a good strong one.

Oil — bottle or spray-can. Permaflote is as good as any (not that any of them are perfect).

Cleaning-aid — I carry a little impregnated pad through which you can run a dry-fly line, both cleaning and slightly oiling it. There's also a dual-purpose one which works for wet and dry lines and for leaders.

Spare nylon — I use a small dispenser, with 6 lb. and 3 lb. nylon spools.

That's about it. The more I fish the less I carry. One fly-box, properly organised should comfortably carry all you need for one day's fishing, including wet flies, dry flies, nymphs, pupae, sedges and whatever. Food and drink I leave in my car, along with heavy bad-weather gear, spare rods and so on. Lugging a box of sandwiches and a flask of coffee (not to mention a hip-flask of whiskey) is going about things the hard way.

Methods — wet-fly
There are some rivers which almost dictate the wet-fly. Fast, stony rivers are made for the method. In general, most Irish rivers and streams have at least some reaches where the wet-fly can be used, particularly in the spring.

There are two basic ways — upstream and across-and-down.

Upstream wet-fly
Useful on smallish rivers, where it enables you to get behind your trout so that he sees you less easily. Best if you can wade. Use a short line and cast upstream or up-and-across, raising the rod as the flies work downstream towards you. Watch for any small movement, which you should be able to see easily as the flies are barely beneath the surface. Strike quickly.

This method is best when the water is not too heavy or deep. It is useful for fishing heavily-brushed streams if you can wade. Learn to use the roll cast and side cast to avoid overhead and bank snags. This method in effect is using straightforward nymphing techniques but of course fished on the blind.

Downstream wet-fly

More accurately across-and-down. Get down low to the edge of the water and cast almost at right angles to the bank. Mend your line upstream quickly to let the flies work without dragging for the first few feet. Trout take at three stages — almost at once when the flies hit the water, when the line straightens in the middle of the cast and finally, when you work the flies back towards you through whatever slack water lies at your bank.

You can fish one, two, three or even four flies. The higher the wind the fewer the flies. Vary your patterns and their sizes and try something out of the ordinary on one of the droppers. The tail fly should have a good entry, while your top dropper or bob can be bushy.

In early spring, the deadliest fly of all is a Black and Silver, which is a very simple dressing of a sparse black hackle, silver ribbing over black body and a few black fibres for a tail. You can add a wing if you please but it is not needed. Worked back slow and deep along a bank in heavy water it clearly imitates a small fish. A Williams Favourite, which has less silver, is almost as good.

It is often difficult to sink your flies in faster water. A leaded or wired Pheasant Tail nymph is useful here. Anyone can tie one. I use copper conductor wire to build up a pronounced thorax or hump at the shoulder and a few pheasant tail fibres for a whisk. There is no need for hackle.

A common mistake which I think is made is to use flies which are too big — indeed, much the same could be said for almost every aspect of Irish trout fishing generally, although anglers are being educated into the ways of smaller fly sizes. I once saw a truly staggering display of thoughtless fly choice — not alone pattern but size — on a small lake where I fished now and then and where the only hope of success were very small lake flies — down to 14 — and more usually fished dry or just in the surface film. Anything bigger was simply ignored by the trout.

One day my solitary boat was joined by another, containing a solitary angler. It began to rain heavily before lunch and the angler, driven ashore by the rain, went off leaving rods behind to wait for a clearance. Coming ashore I took a curious look at his tackle — an enormous dapping rod with a fly of unknown pattern but well over an inch and a half long, its fibres thickly coated with grease, and a monumental wet fly rod of strapping size and armed with three gigantic wet flies of doubtful parentage. Spring salmon might have found them tempting but not these fastidious lake trout.

That is a fault repeated everywhere. How often have I chatted to anglers flogging small waters with flies of a size suitable for salmon. Admittedly in rough and high water, such as you find in early spring, trout will take a larger fly. I used an ancient and bedraggled Black Gnat as a river wet-fly for several years because the first time I hitched its considerable size 8 bulk to the end of my leader in desperation over a blank day I hooked and landed a trout of two pounds, a feat repeated several times afterwards, by which time the gnat, bereft of its glossy wing, was still doing its job mysteriously well. Trout are fickle; by any rights that gnat should have been left alone and spurned.

Larger flies for spring, smaller for summer is a useful general pointer. As a further addendum, I would say that flies between size 14 and 16 are about right, although size 14 can be big enough too. For sedges you can go down to size 9.

Patterns
Wet flies, whether fished up or downstream, imitate nymphs mostly. They also imitate flies hatching in or near the surface, drowned flies swept along by the current and on occasions, other life such as shrimps, waterlice and even small fish.

In theory, the wet-fly angler could bring boxfuls of flies to his work. In practice there is no need to. The following short list of wet-fly patterns has stood me in fine stead over the years and stands firmly after much discarding of dross.

Williams Favourite, Black and Silver Spider, Orange Partridge or Orange Grouse, Gold-Ribbed Hare's Ear, Hackled Greenwell or Greenwell's Glory, March Brown, Red Spinner, Pheasant Tail Nymph (wired or leaded) and a sedge pattern, with possibly a shrimp pattern added. The rail patterns, which are peculiar to Ireland, are good sedge imitations — but I do not approve of killing that vanishing bird the corncrake, from which rail feathers come.

On hindsight, I note that my list is remarkably akin to that of Michael Kennedy whose little booklet *Trout Flies for Irish Waters* is consistently accurate. He too feels little need for an expanded list of wet-flies; my own experience from having boxes of every conceivable pattern and many hardly conceivable at all, is that he is right. All the wet flies you need to fish Irish rivers could comfortably be fitted in a matchbox.

To sum up, the technique of the wet-fly is one primarily for the faster reaches of rivers, whose main thrust is in the spring before the weeds grow too much, and for which a far more limited range of flies is needed than for the dry-fly, the techniques of which demand far more from the angler as far as choice of fly is concerned. The wet-fly angler can simplify matters further by using up to four different patterns on the one cast — and could easily work his way through his entire range of patterns in half an hour, whereas it might take a day or two for the dryfly man to do the same.

This is not to say that wet-fly fishing is easier than dry-fly. Indeed I now believe (once having believed the opposite) that the truly fine wet-fly angler is a better fisherman than his dry-fly counterpart. To gain the most from his technique, the wet-fly angler must have a sense of touch or feel such as is beyond the dry-fly user. This is why the tool of the trade, the wet-fly rod, must be sensitive and responsive. Unlike the dry-fly rod, which does not have to *sense* out the fish the wet-fly rod is an extension of the fly working at the end of the leader — and an extension of feeling for the angler.

To watch a great wet-fly angler in operation is to view something almost uncanny. On the River Nore below the lovely Norman village of Inistioge in Kilkenny, I watched an old man knee deep in that rushing current bring trout after trout to the bag without apparently striking each fish. So fine was his sense of feel that I, fishing near him, felt only the odd touch, landing one fish to his five. I have improved since then and like to think myself a competent hand with a wet-fly rod. But I have not the razored touch of the fully-accomplished in the art. That is achieved only by the few — and of that few, most highly by those whose life has been lived for wet-fly.

The best material still for wet-fly rods is split cane. It has a touch no other material has. It need not be long — nine feet or even up to ten. It should be almost floppy in action, with a pronounced droop from butt to tip when sighted along. Its action should be slow and deliberate, just like the wet-fly caster's.

Every angler has his own way of making up a leader or — as it is doggedly called in Ireland — a cast. Mine is nine to ten feet, with two droppers, usually of a stronger breaking strain than the part of the leader where they hang. Droppers need to stand out from the main leader so that the flies do not get wrapped around the latter and are allowed to work properly in the current, weaving and sidling. Keep between two and three feet between the flies. You don't have to use more than one if you don't want to; in a wind, one is often the only way you can fish safely without tangling or getting an errant fly whipping you in the face.

While the dry-fly will always have my full heart, I like the wet-fly. There are rivers which demand it as their due. It does not bring, I would say, as large an average size of trout as does the dry-fly. But for all that it is a great and honoured favourite with the Irish river angler.

Dry-fly tactics

Although you can use the dry-fly more or less throughout the angling year on most Irish rivers, it has always been very much a secondary method with Irish river anglers who as a race, are devoted to the wet-fly in much the same way as that method holds sway yet over most river anglers in northern Britain.

In recent years however, the dry-fly has made significant inroads, cutting deep into tradition. Hardly surprising when it is a method of much wider practical use than is the wet-fly which although the better way of catching fish in the spring waters, thereafter is limited severely by weed and low water.

The best of the dry-fly fishing is on the limestone streams, both big and small. Many limestone streams, particularly in the flat midlands, are slow-running waters, heavily weeded, but holding small numbers of large trout; they are ideal for dry-fly.

These limestone streams, if they have recovered from drainage, provide reliable hatches of fly-life — large dark olives, iron blues, blue-winged olives and pale wateries being the most prominent and therefore useful. In addition they have large hatches of sedges — day-flying sedges such as the grey flag being particularly important — alders and others.

The spring provides perhaps the liveliest action. In late March and April the large dark olives hatch for an hour or two around midday and often provoke a surprisingly sustained rise of fish. The iron blue, which follows conveniently on the large dark olive, is a favourite of trout and has given me some of my most memorable days. The spring and early summer fishing is built around those two species of *baetis* and no angler should be without suitable imitations.

The summer fishing poses very different problems. For one thing, daytime hatches have become so sporadic that often rivers seem lifeless — and riseless — for days on end. I regard summer — perhaps a little sweepingly — as being a time for evening rather than daytime fishing; and so it is dealt with in the next chapter.

The key to successful daytime angling is to know your natural flies and their times of emergence. It is a never-ending source of surprise to me that more anglers do not take the trouble to learn even the few basic facts which will see them through. A good rise of fish is a rare enough event to ensure that anglers lucky enough to come across one should be fully knowledgeable to take best advantage of it. And yet, and yet . . . .

Anglers can make their own individual choice as to how to fish the dry-fly. Is it to fish the rise or fish the river blank — "fishing on the blind" as it accurately is known? Most assuredly he is lucky who finds trout rising continuously on his rivers; more often it is the blank surface which greets the angler.

Invertebrate drift

I am hesitant about introducing too much academic-seeming theory into angling, which has an unerring knack of upsetting such ordinances. At the same time, there is in the life of a river which feeds the trout a certain basic pattern of behaviour. And it behoves the angler to know something of it.

The invertebrate life of a river, such as many types of nymphs, larvae, shrimp and so on has peaks and valleys of activity, just as has a human or a cow. Most rest and feed at different times of the day — by day I mean 24 hours. What the angler must remember is that *the activity in feeding of the trout is related directly to the feeding habits of its invertebrate prey.*

The point is such a momentous one that I do not hesitate to enlarge upon it. If you are inclined away from rather than towards scientific explanations of how trout food behaves, turn on a few pages.

Most invertebrates live off tiny brown and green algae in a river, which in turn grow mainly on the tops of stones where there is most light. Many young nymphs (mostly either crawlers or burrowers) live mostly on the tops of stones but as they grow, tend to hide more and more under the stones — in other words, further and further away from their main source of food, the algae on the upper part of the stones.

This is easily checked. Turn up the stones in most rivers during daytime and you will see plenty of life — but mostly *underneath* the stones.

Scientific research has shown that the intensity of light decides how an invertebrate largely behaves. Temperature also plays a part — more of them move about in warm weather. Simplifying a complex scientific argument, each animal's internal biological clock determines how it behaves; neurohormones building up during the daylight hours are released when darkness comes, alerting the animal which then becomes active. At this time, when the light is going or gone, invertebrates move from under the stones to feed above.

Why this happens is clear scientifically. Nature, on the other hand, feels apparently that as the invertebrates are easy meat for predators such as trout in the daytime, they are better protected by darkness, when the trout sees less. Hence the complex set of behavioural patterns which cause the animal to emerge at night, feed during darkness and retreat back to the safety of its lair once light comes again.

This behaviour is responsible for what scientists call invertebrate drift. There are two sorts of invertebrate drift, voluntary and involuntary. As the animals move out and up to feed, some get caught in the current and drift downstream. Others involuntarily allow themselves to be carried thus for reasons of their own — possibly food shortage, pollution, or even water shortage.

For these and other reasons, invertebrate activity is highest at dusk, when the animals move out to feed and drift down in the current, and right through the night, at the end of which they try to move back in under the stones and weed cover.

The trout's reaction to this increase in the food quantity available to him is predictable. He becomes active when the invertebrates do. But as he cannot see well enough in the dark, he feeds on these invertebrates when there is light enough for him to catch them — at dusk and dawn, just before they move back into sheltering cover.

Thus the river trout is most active at dusk and dawn — simply because his main food does likewise. It stands to simple reason therefore, that the times where the angler is likely to be most successful are at dusk and dawn. Hence the relative superiority of evening fishing during the summer, when the activity of invertebrates is supported by the pattern of evening hatches. A double meal for the trout, so to speak.

I have lingered on this theory of invertebrate drift simply because it has revolutionised my own approach to evening and dawn fishing. I do very little dawn fishing, being a poor early riser. But I am not saying too much, nor going too far, when I claim that a grasp of how the trout's food behaves has immeasurably increased not alone the pleasure I get from angling, but my understanding of what I am doing and why — and the same for the trout.

If I have seemed to dwell too much on this point, it is because I believe it to be so utterly central to success — not success merely in terms of fish caught but in that ultimate satisfaction of interpreting

a complex set of conditions and through knowledge and awareness, conquering them.

Let us now translate this knowledge into catching fish on the dry-fly during daylight.

Spring and summer mornings start early. So do the trout. But early morning is a time when really just one major fly hatches — caenis. Trout feed well at this time but are very hard to catch. Which brings me to another belief — that the low-level light of early morning and late evening appears to magnify signs of danger for the trout. Is it the slanting light catching too well the line or the leader? Perhaps; we cannot be certain. But every angler who has fished these two periods knows only too sorrowfully the familiar sight of alarmed trout arrowing out ahead of him.

Caenis fishing in early morning is tremendously challenging. So for that matter is getting up early enough to be there for the rise; but it is worth it in the cool softness of these stilled mornings.

In this part of the world — that is, in western Europe — the techniques of caenis or midge fishing which have so revolutionised American stream-fishing remain undeveloped. A six-foot rod, a 1 lb. leader, a size 22 or even 24 fly — these are tactics and tackle to match the caenis challenge. I have seen American anglers visiting Ireland try out their methods and they work. We have, so far anyway, been too hidebound by far to discard our normal dry-fly tackle for the caenis approach.

The message either way is use the smallest and lightest tackle you have. Keep your fly on the water over a rising fish and put it on his nose. He does not have to move far for a feed of caenis and he is not going to move to accept your offering. You may well find you have to cast thirty, forty, even fifty or more times over a single rising fish before he takes it — if he takes it. So the fish you pick should be big and worth all the trouble.

An alternative, and a last-ditch effort of desperation, is to try a big bushy fly thrown in amongst his tiny cousins. It occasionally but very sporadically works. I have caught trout during a dawn rise of caenis by using a daddylonglegs. But it is cheating a little. Goddard's Last Hope is a goodish pattern, but really any small, whitish Pale Watery pattern will do. Do not be afraid to sink it in the surface.

OPPOSITE:
The River Liffey at Straffan, County Kildare. In its middle reaches the Liffey is an excellent limestone water but is heavily fished and is subject to abrupt rises and falls in water-level due to the workings of a major waterworks at its headwaters. It holds some very big trout and is also a good coarse fish water.

Daytime fishing other than at dawn is a relatively simple affair. Simply follow the hatch of whatever is hatching, be it large dark olives, iron blues, grey flags or whatever. If there is no hatch, fish the dry-fly on the blind. This is surprisingly effective and I never cease to marvel at the number of trout willing to have a cut at a fly floated randomly over their slumbrous noses.

Nymphing

Nymphing is a technique mostly of the summer months when daytime rises are few. On Irish rivers, the technique is so little removed from that of the upstream wet-fly that I hesitate almost to separate the two. But it is fair to say that in nymphing, the nymph should go deeper than the upstream wet-fly; and that while the latter is designed for trout "on the fin" and high in the water, the former method is largely to tempt trout lying deep.

I have tried many nymphs and now confine myself to two — a leaded or wired Pheasant Tail and a creation of my own, a leaded or wired Green Nymph, which I dress with silver wire to build up a thorax, thickly ribbing the body with green tying silk and finally tying in a sloping slip of a wing, which can be from almost any brown feathers. The silver shows through the body attractively and the wing helps the nymph to work and vibrate with the current. This pattern can represent a number of nymphs but I suspect also that trout sometimes take it for a small fish.

In nymphing on Irish rivers, it is rare enough for the angler to see his fish. This is not to say that he is fishing blind; more likely is he to know that there is a trout where he casts and that the trout is a worthwhile fellow. The number of times the angler will see the trout take the nymph must be tiny. So he fishes by feel and instinctive touch — the hallmark of the natural angler. And the better the touch and feel, the better the angler.

Remember to pitch the nymph well upstream of the trout to give it time to sink to the level of his nose when it reaches him. A swift current often sweeps a nymph along at surprisingly shallow depths; you must allow for that. Watch the water for a flicker or a hump or that slight disturbance which always comes with a taking trout moving to his food. If there is none visible to your eye, watch the leader; and strike at the least movement.

Nymphing is above all, about watchfulness and instinct. It is a difficult art — perhaps one of the hardest in angling. But in the daytime during July and August in particular it may be the only way in which you will take trout.

Chapter Eight

Evening Tactics

The evening rise — the Blue-Winged Olive — marking a fish — a good trout caught — tale of two trout — the light problem

> *Oh, what a tangled cast we weave*
> *When first we practice to deceive*
> *The wary trout;*
> *But if we're made of proper stuff,*
> *and practice hard and long enough*
> *'Twill straighten out.*

Celina, *Fishing Gazette*

H. T. SHERINGHAM, once angling editor of *The Field*, in his *Memories and Morals*, has delightfully summed-up the frustrations of fishing the evening rise. In a passage where he resolves to act upon the advice of Frederick Halford, the so-called father of the dry-fly, and remain calm and collected during the short hour or so when the trout begin to rise as we imagine they should, Sheringham finds himself rushing feverishly up and down the river bank, fumblingly changing flies the while. In the end his anxiety overcomes him and the evening passes largely fishless; once more he has bungled it.

So it is with most of us. We know that if conditions are anyway right at all, the trout should properly behave in a certain way. In other words, the flies will hatch and hopefully there will be trout to eat them — and ours.

But the evening rise imposes strictures on us which no other angling period does. We know we have perhaps an hour or so when there will be blue-winged olives hatching and perhaps some spinners on the water, or the pale evening dun will be about. An hour, if you think about it, is ample time to land three or four good fish, allowing for all the extraneous interferences which bedevil angling. But so often we get it wrong.

Evening fishing begins sometime in the latter half of May and ends

in September. Its peak is late June and July. By August, the rivers
are often so low and so denuded of oxygen that the fish are
disinclined utterly to move to surface fly. But July, so much reviled
by the angler of the daytime, can often be a very good month indeed,
especially on those limestone streams where there are consistent
hatches of blue-winged olives and sedges.

Evening fishing is very much a question of getting things
absolutely right. If you know your river and its moods, you will know
those particular stretches where the blue-winged olive hatches
regularly. Be there — and do not move. Do not above all be tempted
by rising trout far above you or immediately below you; concentrate
on your chosen stretch and fish the rise when it comes.

When I first fished my favourite local river, I was aware that
drainage had wrecked it and that while the trout were back, I did not
know how many there were. On a July evening of calm sunset I found
out. There was a perfect frenzy as they fought to gulp down the blue-
winged olives — oddly enough a splendid hatch whose density I have
not seen repeated. Their frenzy transmitted itself to me; I miscast,
got tangled, caught myself and my rod in the reeds and rushes, fell
down banks, was eaten by midges, put fish down one after the other,
pulled the hook out of others and reached that stage of incoherent
anger where I would willingly have cried with rage. And not a fish
landed.

Contrast this with an evening a season or two ago. I had marked
down a rising fish in a narrow run between two banks of tall flags. To
reach him, I had to cast my fly some fifteen yards directly upstream;
he lay in about two feet or so of swift water with no more than
eighteen inches between the banks of flags. There would be one cast
— and it would have to be not just right, but utterly, totally,
absolutely right.

It was. The Blue-Winged Olive landed two feet above his nose.
The fight was predictable; I bustled him downstream and held him
tight in a deep hole at my feet and within a couple of minutes his two-
pound weight was in my net. He had not been so much caught as
ambushed.

I find a wonderful satisfaction in such catches, where the set of
angling circumstances is largely against the angler. Oddly enough
the next outing after that one had a similar result. I decided to fish a
stretch of slow-running river which was full of pike and perch but
which I reasoned must hold a trout or two worth the catching. I
walked upstream for two miles or more, over barbed-wire fences,
through drainage ditches, fields of cabbages and corn and saw not a

rise. Then, a hundred yards upstream, I saw a fish feeding steadily and intently.

I reconnoitred with great care. He lay in the middle of a wide, smooth stretch of river, just above a dip where the current buckled smoothly over a limestone ledge underwater. So eager was his feeding that his back was frequently out of the water — and what a back! But this was a fiendish cast; I could not wade this deep water and so must put a fly again about fifteen yards up and across into smooth water. My line and part of the leader would fall in faster water and within a yard of landing the fly would drag.

Distance and placing were vital. I lengthened line across the river and put the fly a foot above his head and about six inches to one side. He took with instant confidence and surged right across the river to my bank with tremendous power. But the odds were against him; there was water to spare and I had him on the bank within five minutes. Three pounds two ounces — my best fish from that river. And he was the only fish I saw the entire evening.

I instance these two fish and how they were caught because they are a reflection of how I fish the evening rise today. I mark my fish down and pursue them to the exclusion of others.

Let me tell you another story — against myself. I had marked down two good feeding fish in a little pool and for many evenings had tried to catch them. Such were the vagaries of current that to avoid drag was next to impossible. The technical questions set by the water, the strained way in which I had to stand to cast, and the feeding patterns of the trout themselves made an overall problem of impressive difficulty. And it found me wanting.

And yet this is the sort of problem I most enjoy. I determined to get at least one of these fish. They would feed on the surface for three or four minutes, one three yards behind the other, and then go down. Instantly a trail of bubbles would come to the surface. They were grubbing for shrimps or nymphs in the weeds about three feet down. This would go on for three or four minutes and then they would re-surface to feed on floating fly or nymphal life which they had disturbed underwater. The pattern was always the same, evening after evening.

I was not without some success. Several evenings I pricked one or other of them. The disturbance they made then showed me how big they were. I tried to catch the lower one, figuring that this would not alarm the upper one who must be the bigger by all the standards of trout behaviour. But this lower one lay in such a way that no cast could prevent drag.

The solution I found was to wait until the trout were rising vigorously and then by casting short and often, keep the fly on the water even for a foot or two before it dragged. Several times the lower fish rose and missed; and then he came at it determinedly and I had him. He rushed upstream with great strength; but there was in his pulling something which forewarned me. Sure enough he had been hooked in the dorsal fin and at about half a pound, was most assuredly not one of the big fish which had occupied so many of my evenings. And of course the pool was disturbed.

I did, weeks later, catch the upper one who weighed just over two and a half pounds. In the end, a Coachman put on his nose fatally tempted him. But I will long remember the extreme problems both trout set for me.

Evening fishing, then, is not at all easy. The thing to remember is to keep calm and to pick your fish and fish for it and it only. Find that stretch where hatches are consistent and take your pitch there. The main hatches on limestone streams will be of blue-winged olives, pale wateries and pale evening duns, with some sedges. Late at night trout will take sedges of surprising clumsiness and size but earlier on, especially in low water, you will need fine leaders and small flies — sizes 16 and 18 I find suitable.

Be aware too, of the problem of light. There are stretches of water on all rivers where the angle of the evening light alerts trout to the fact that they are being fished for. How exactly this happens I do not know; but happen it does. There is really very little you can do about it; no matter how lightly your leader falls, it appears as though to the trout you have deposited a ton of TNT on their noses. They respond with those familiar arrowing rushes upstream to safety. Pass these stretches by and resolve to teach them a lesson during the daylight hours.

Fly Patterns

I find I have restricted myself to those few flies which fish consistently well for me. As with so much in fishing, fly selection is largely a question of confidence. But here is my short list for what it is worth for dry-fly in the evening.

Blue-Winged Olive and Orange Quill for the hatching dun; Sherry Spinner for the BWO spinner; Pale Watery, tied spent, for pale evening duns and most small pale wateries; Tups Indispensable, tied lightly and with a very lightly-coloured hackle; Coachman — a wonderful evening fly in June; Alder, a largish pattern which can imitate most sedges in the evening; and a Red Spinner, which can sometimes be effective when all else fails.

This is a very short list indeed but I find it works for me. You could add perhaps a Black Gnat if you wish. The spent pattern of Pale Watery, which is really an imitation of the Pale Evening Dun, is a strip of white feather tied spent, with red tying silk for the body — a very simple pattern but deadly during high summer evenings. A most effective fly for limestone waters, designed by Dick Harris.

Evening fishing, while it often provokes a violent reaction from the trout, has a similar effect on the fisherman. It is frustrating and irritating and often fruitless. But it does offer a very real challenge to the angler who wants himself set a technical problem of magnitude. Take it all in all, it is the most satisfying way to fish the dry-fly for trout.

The River Barrow near Borris in County Carlow. A river of great contrast, the Barrow has some stretches which rival the brown trout angling on any river in Ireland. Elsewhere it is either polluted as it passes through the numerous towns along its length or is coarse fish water — specifically big pike water. Its faster reaches afford splendid trout fishing.

Irish lake boats such as these two are wide, strong and lengthy — and often need all three qualities in the wild waters of the west, where the great limestone lakes can become inland seas. Two anglers can fly-fish comfortably in these boats, with a middle angler dapping or just handling the oars. Tholepins are safer to use than rowlocks but all oars should be tied down.

——————— ○ ———————

SECTION THREE

——————— ○ ———————

The Rainbow Trout

——————————— ○ ———————————

Chapter Nine

Rainbow Trout

A new phenomenon — their neglect — good future — some rainbow lakes — feeding habits — tactics — useful patterns — the dry -fly

> *And angling, too, that solitary vice,*
> *Whatever Isaac Walton sings or says;*
> *The quaint old cruel coxcomb in his gullet*
> *Should have a hook and a small trout to pull it*

Byron, Don Juan

RAINBOW trout are relatively new in Ireland. They arc also infrequent and while many Irish lake anglers will have fished for them at some stage, there are comparatively few who fish for them regularly, largely because of the sparse distribution of the species.

For that and other reasons, rainbows are somewhat neglected in Ireland. There are very few rainbow lakes as such and no rainbow rivers in the true sense. The development of rainbow fishing, such as it is, has been done by the Central Fisheries Board, formerly the Inland Fisheries Trust, and has been limited to such counties as Sligo (Loch na Leibe); Galway (Lough Acalla) and Westmeath (White Lake). There are other lakes with rainbows including Annagh in County Cavan, but these three are the principal ones. In Cork, a number of small lakes have been stocked with rainbows also.

In rivers, rainbows are limited to those into which they have escaped from fish farms situated on the river. This has led to some interesting fishing on several streams in Wicklow; but for the rest, rainbows are non-existent in most Irish rivers.

The attitude of most Irish trout fishermen must account for the lack of rainbow fishing development. The rainbow is regarded as being inferior to the native brown. He probably is in some ways, being particularly difficult to breed in the wild; but there is no doubt that he is a much superior stocked specimen than the brown trout. My own experience of Irish rainbows leads me to think that the stocked rainbow is both sharper and a harder fighter than the stocked brown trout. Certain it is that he is much maligned as a fish in Irish waters, except by those who relish the different challenge which the rainbow offers to the angler.

The slow development of rainbows in Ireland is even less comprehensible in the light of the shaky foundations of much of the country's trout fishing. More and more loch and river fisheries are coming under tremendous pressure — from over-fishing, from pollution, from drainage, from water-abstraction schemes. The great lakes of the west and midlands, though still good by the standards of other European countries, are a shallow imitation of what they once were. The future of Irish trout angling surely lies in the development of the many hundreds of small lakes and reservoirs, where management can control exactly what happens to the waters and where fishing development is easier and less costly than on larger sheets of water.

For this type of fishery — almost unknown in Ireland — the rainbow is a better choice than the brown trout, if only on a put-and-take basis. It is also untrue that the rainbow, if unchecked, will eliminate the brown trout if the two share the same water. There is room for both; the experience on the White Lake in County Westmeath which admittedly has probably some of the best feeding of any lake in Ireland, would appear to confirm that they can live together.

I have little doubt that in a few years, the best lake fishing for trout in Ireland will be on small, tightly-managed fisheries operated by syndicates or clubs which stock the lakes and look after the fishing. Ireland is well suited to this; at the time of writing, I am one of the original members of a syndicate which I believe to be the first in this country — other than in the North of Ireland — to acquire fishing rights on a small private lake and to start to develop it as a trout fishery. I have little doubt that it will be the first of many; we have only to look at the British experience to see that.

Rainbows so far, apart from a few technical/genetic problems, have adapted singularly well to Irish waters. They feed well and grow much faster than brown trout. If the water is deep enough, they over-winter well also. However, spawning remains a daunting problem; and of course rainbows seem to desert rivers as soon as they are put into it or escape into it as the case may be. One of the more interesting aspects of the Wicklow rivers into which farm-bred rainbows have escaped is that the rainbows appear not to desert the river too quickly.

For the moment though, rainbows remain very much a put-and-take fish. This is not to say that they require replacing every year; if they have overwintered well, rainbows can survive several years in Irish waters. But if they grow more quickly than the native brown trout, they also mature and die off much more quickly; four years of age is a rainbow's life-span.

As a fast growing, quickly-maturing fish, the rainbow requires a lot of food. He will not get this in acidic lakes and so needs the rich feeding of limestone waters to keep him happy. Three such lakes are the prime rainbow lakes in Ireland — Loch na Leibe in the Sligo hills, Lough Acalla in the flat stonewalled countryside of Galway — and what an unusual lake that is — and the deeply-blued waters of the White Lake in the low limestone hills of County Westmeath.

Such is the feeding on these lakes that the rainbows rarely find the need to come to the surface unless the hatch of fly is such as to outweigh the choice on the bottom or in mid-water. The young crayfish and perch fry abounding in the White Lake, for instance, are a rainbow's delight. Add to this diet a dessert of shrimps, corixae, waterlice, snails and various nymphs and the picture is an even clearer one. At most times during the fishing season, rainbows will be feeding deep.

Tactics

Rainbows have some habits which are different from those of trout. They shoal in sometimes surprisingly large numbers and they feed less on the surface and more on the bottom. They appear less discriminating in their choice of fly pattern, occasionally taking lures such as streamers and perch-fry imitations which would deter most Irish brown trout. On the whole they demand a different approach by the angler who must use the tactics which have become so successful on British stillwaters — deep-sinking lures, nymphs and streamers which are as foreign to the Irish angler as the rainbow is to Irish waters.

My own experience of rainbow fishing in Ireland has led me to think, somewhat tentatively, that rainbow angling is best at very specific times. They will often feed very heavily at dawn on caenis and such spent fly as is left on the water from the previous night. They will rise reasonably frequently at around mid-day to whatever is going — one rising rainbow will sometimes tend to touch off an accompanying shoal to do the same thing, although to the angler's eyes there is often no increase in surface fly to justify such a rise. And rainbows will feed in the evening, patrolling water some distance offshore to pick up spent flies and emergent sedges. They are good cruisers, and in this respect echo the habits of many bigger brown trout.

I have found, after much barren trial, that traditional methods such as casting from the drifting boat need rethinking when it comes to rainbows. It is best to try to locate a shoal or at the very least to make an educated guess as to where the rainbows might be feeding. It is, needless to say, easier to do this on a small lake than on a bigger one; and if you fish such a small lake frequently, you will quickly get to know the good spots. Over these spots you must either drift slowly or anchor. Then using deepwater tactics, you start fishing.

For this I use a deep-sinking line, usually with a leader of at least 10 to 12 feet, and with two droppers. I use bigger flies than normal for lake trout — but then I tend to use small flies anyway. I vary the size of my flies at the beginning — say from a size 8 up to a size 14; and I vary the pattern equally. Allow the line and flies to sink and then begin the retrieve- varying the speed, sometimes smooth, sometimes jerky.

It is impossible properly to list or short-list, a selection of flies suitable for Irish rainbows. Of the more traditional patterns, Claret and Mallard, Wickham's,Invicta and Dunkeld I find effective. New patterns are legion — you pays your money and very definitely its your own choice. I find that the Missionary works well, as does the Whiskey fly; and even Chief Nebedah, that extravagantly-dressed exotic, has his day, as do the various dressings of the Muddlcr Minnow (although why an Irish rainbow trout should take an imitation of the American cockatush minnow defies rationale).

Simplifying the choice of pattern, I would say that a cast of three flies should include a nymphal imitation, such as a leaded Pheasant Tail Nymph, or if not a shrimp or corixae pattern. Snails can be imitated by a Black and Peacock Spider. Any of the large fancy patterns, such as Whiskey flies, may well be held to imitate perch fry and uphold this thinking by doing well in shallow waters, where the perch fry congregate. Muddlers, which are surface-fished, I fancy are taken for big sedges. And other big fancy flies fished very deep and slowly may well be taken for young crayfish.

Dry-fly works well for rainbows at certain times. The Daddylonglegs has got many fish for me and I find it almost the best weapon to use during those irritating rises of caenis. Midge pupae should not be left out — rainbows feed heavily on them almost every day and you need several imitations, including green and orange-based patterns. Wickham and Invicta, fished either wet or in the surface film, are effective sedge imitations but rainbows also take Green Peters and Murroughs well during the evening. Do not either be without a Black Gnat.

I am conscious of the roughness of this list. But such is the unformed nature of rainbow fishing in Ireland that much of it, including the most effective choice of fly pattern, remains ill-defined.

The great British angler Richard Walker with an enormous rainbow from one of Britain's prime fisheries, Avington. The stocked rainbow has become the staple target for most British stillwater anglers and Ireland, which is facing many of the same problems of pollution, angling pressure and many more, may well see itself turning to this hard-fighting and quick-growing fish as the answer to the future.

———— o ————

SECTION FOUR

———— o ————

The White Trout

———————— o ————————

A good white trout from a west of Ireland fishery, where in general the fish run smaller than along Ireland's other and richer coasts. Irish white trout flies include many of those favoured elsewhere but have a sprinkling of special tyings for specific waters, including the Delphi Silver, Costelloe Blue and Silver, the Yellow Dyson and many others.

Preparing to net a good white trout in Lough Currane, County Kerry. Currane, with its free fishing for white trout and salmon, is perhaps the single finest white trout lake in Ireland. But its large size and changing geography, allied to the preferences which its fish show for particular lies in the lake make local knowledge essential if a visiting angler is to catch fish. Currane regularly produces its

Chapter Ten

The White Trout

Loch, river and tidal fishing — Currane — the West — early white
trout — too traditional — netting overkill — Connemara — how the
white trout behaves — their life and times — running fish —
summing it up

Casus ubique valet; semper tibi pendeat hamus;
quo minime credis gurgite piscis erit.
(There's aye a chance; keep casting on and see
In swirl where least you think a fish will be)

Ovid, Ars Amat.

Y ou betray a certain lack of sensibility if in Ireland you refer to
the white trout as a sea trout. For in this land of white trout he
is whiter than white and is known by no other name, whether
sewin or peal or even sea trout.

Ireland is not exactly a land of white trout either; but it is very
close to it. For every coastal county has its share of rivers, and some
of lochs and lochans where the white trout runs. And even in such a
small island you will find such different emphases in the fishing for
white trout as will bewilder you.

Basically there are three ways to fish for white trout in Ireland.
There is loch or lake fishing, which is confined mostly, if not entirely,
to the western seaboard; there is river fishing, which is generally
distributed around the coast, although its quality varies a good deal
more, and finally there is angling in tidal and brackish waters,
whether estuarine or the sea itself.

By far the best-known, and most widely practiced of these three is
the classic form of Irish white trout fishing — the loch fishing of the
western seaboard, the cream of which is in Kerry, Connemara,
Mayo and Donegal. The fact that those areas are very similar —
mostly mountainous, with spate rivers which run off rapidly but
which frequently have a network of lochs attached to their courses —
is no accident. They are white trout country *par excellence*.

Other than Lough Currane near Waterville in County Kerry, Connemara's consistently good white trout fishing is probably the best in the country. Currane is something unto itself, a lake of distinct individuality, larger than any other white trout lake, with bigger than average fish. All in all, I would consider it the best lake for white trout in Ireland, vying with two or three of the smaller Connemara lochs and one or two in Mayo, but getting the vote because its fish are generally much bigger than the fairly low-sized fish that Connemara offers.

Other than loch fishing, the other two aspects of white trout angling in Ireland — saltwater/estuarine fishing, and river fishing — are curiously neglected. In Donegal, river fishing predominates but in Connemara and Mayo the lochs rule almost unchallenged. And if there is a generalisation to be made around the country, it surely is that if the white trout angler can fish a loch in preference to a river he will do it.

Saltwater and estuarine waters are almost completely ignored and such white trout as are caught by anglers in these places are, I suspect, largely accidental. I find this hard to understand. I began my own white trout fishing in saltwater, fishing the mouth of a small river in the south-east corner of Ireland, where on the flooding tide the white trout came questing for sandeels over the sand flats. A ledgered sandeel brought us such fish as I have rarely seen since, averaging three to four pounds in weight. I took this as normal, as children will (I would have been about twelve years old); today I know better.

Hugh Falkus, that most knowledgeable of white trout fishers and writers, experimented very successfully with saltwater fishing for white trout both during and after he lived in Ireland. Not alone did he show what could be done but he showed clearly what potential there was in using a commonsense approach to saltwater angling. Yet I can think of scarcely more than a handful of people around the country who do now what he did then, angle for white trout outside the strict parameter of loch and river. I don't do it myself; but then I live far from the sea and my white trout angling these days is limited to a few days in the autumn.

Partly I think one reason for such lamentable failure to make the most of white trout fishing in Ireland is due to the fact that so much of the more traditional methods of loch fishing is still reasonably successful enough to dissuade diehard anglers from experimenting. Most Irish white trout anglers see no reason to change if the fishing they get is already good enough. And I suspect that until the day comes when this is no longer the case, they will continue to fish as before.

In fact, looked at in this way, white trout angling in Ireland has changed remarkably little over the years, other than being of lower quality and increasingly restricted by illegal drift netting which, particularly along parts of the western seaboard, is manifestly both unfair and a disgrace. No angler worthy of that title begrudges the netman his living but the wholesale and profligate raping of the white trout shoals and stock is an unthinking and selfish death-hold, perpetrated for the most part illegally. There are documented cases of drift nets of five, six and even seven *miles* long being used along the west coast. That such action is illegal goes without saying; that it is tolerated not by the law but by the public generally is a shameful reflection.

There are numerous lakes and small lochs in Ireland which provide white trout fishing of variable quality. But Connemara, that strange and beguiling region on the western seaboard of Galway, is surely the king of the domain.

Connemara's geographical formation provides the key to its breadth of quality white trout angling. The mountain ranges to the east — the Twelve Bens in particular — trap the rain-clouds sweeping in from the Atlantic ocean, feeding a thousand streams and runnels on the steep slopes, which in turn drain off to fill the many larger river systems which vein the lower coastal plain. Connemara is a rainy place; and if this does not suit the non-fishing tourist, it is a great blessing indeed for the angler.

Rain is not of course, the whole answer. After all, it falls plentifully in this western coast. But Connemara's river systems are almost unique in having tagged on to them as it were, numerous lochs of varying sizes which not alone act as reservoirs but almost as dams in holding water levels and preventing spate water from running off as quickly as it might otherwise do. And the lochs also act as reservoirs or holding pools for the fish.

As Kingsmill Moore shrewdly pointed out, the peat which clothes the rocky ribs of the Connemara coastal plain does its own job in holding back and filtering through the heavy falls of rainwater which thunder down from the hills. The peat, acting as does a sponge, holds water and only gradually releases it into the streams, rivers and lochs. Thus the water level of Connemara's white trout freshwater rivers and lochs is remarkably stable given the volatile nature of its spate rivers.

Add to this stability the ebb and flood of tidal waters at the mouth of the numerous white trout rivers and the picture is complete of an ingenious if complex natural mechanism which assures for much of the season a plenitude of fish and generally reasonable water conditions in which to catch them.

All of course, is not perfect. Although very little thorough research has been done on the locationary nature of the white trout, such as where exactly he wanders during the time he is not in the river, there is today a general and hardening agreement that in fact he wanders very little indeed and spends that time feeding around the coast. The western coast of Ireland is not noticeable for its rich feeding grounds; and this, I suspect, accounts largely for the generally small size of the Connemara white trout. Frequently a day's catch will average perhaps three-quarters of a pound — herling in other words; and generally speaking the western white trout is a very junior brother to his stalwart eastern cousin. Currane, of course, is the great exception.

Most of the loch fishing for white trout is done from boats. Shore fishing is possible on most if not all lochs; but I feel, as with brown trout, that the shore angler is unnecessarily restricting himself by comparison with the boat angler. Irish lochs are often heavily reeded; some are perfectly fishable in that they allow the shore angler to cast as far as he can. But many of the best holding areas for loch white trout are often far from the shore and can be covered only with a boat. By all means work away from the shore but remember that you are handicapping yourself very severely. And most water which can be fished from the shore can also be fished from a boat.

Although many Irish white trout lochs are very small indeed and often have few boats on them (Clogher, one of the best in Connemara, has just one boat) this does not mean that you will find white trout all over a loch. You will not; instead you may find that each loch, however small, has its good and bad spots. White trout are a shoaling fish and show distinct preferences for favourite lies not necessarily for all of that time they are in a loch, but even during changes in water levels, temperatures, atmospheric conditions and conditions of water.

It hardly needs pointing out that the angler must find out where the fish are if he is to catch them. On a biggish loch, such as Lough Currane, a strange angler would be lost and would find the holding grounds and favourite white trout lies purely by accident. That job is only marginally easier in the small lochs of Connemara, for instance; even a loch of ten or twenty acres needs thorough searching before the angler can be sure where the white trout are.

A knowledge then, not alone of how the white trout behaves but why it behaves thus does the angler no harm at all.

White trout can be compared to salmon in that they are migratory. Their purpose in running up into freshwater is to spawn in the topmost streams. Young fish leave fresh water for saltwater usually in spring or early summer, by which time they can be anything from one to five years old, although Connemara fish by some accounts are nearly all quite young fish when they leave freshwater. When white trout have been a year, or even two to three years feeding off the coast, they return to spawn.

White trout spawn around the end of October right through November and unlike salmon, often survive the first spawning to spawn several or even many times. These two factors — the ability to spawn several times and the varied years they spend at sea — mean that white trout vary widely in size. In a typical Connemara catch, the majority will be smallish fish of under or about a pound but it is quite possible to have several fish of three to four pounds. Salmon, on the other hand, tend to be largely of one size in individual fisheries particularly in the west of Ireland.

Many white trout may be very small indeed, often down to half a pound or so. These are the fish which having left the river in early spring as young fish, return again later in the year, usually in late August and early September; because they are immature fish, not many spawn. To the serious white trout angler, these herling are an inveterate nuisance, since they are really too small to keep, although many white trout anglers do kill them. Basically the white trout the angler wants to catch are those who have spent at least a year at sea, by which time they are at least a pound in weight.

Runs of white trout vary very much in Ireland, as do the sizes of the fish. The time of year at which they run varies too. In Connemara few anglers fish for white trout seriously before July, although I have several times seen quite big fish moving upriver as early as June. July is the peak month, particularly in the lower stretches of Connemara fisheries, which are often a complex network of rivers and lochs, up which a run of white trout is governed almost exclusively by water conditions. The very top lochs on some systems, such as Shanawona on Fermoyle (beloved of Kingsmill Moore) and Tawnyard on the Erriff fish better later in the year, particularly if the summer has been a dry one with not enough water to carry the fish right up through the lower part of the system to the upper part.

As I have said, water conditions are vital in white trout fishing. Not alone do fish need the actual body of heavier water to allow them to make their way upriver — there appears to be something in the taste and smell of fresh water after heavy rain which spurs some impulse to run. Anyone who has watched a shoal of white trout drought-bound in a river pool or small loch and seen their reaction as floodwater percolates downriver will know what I mean; the fish rush about excitedly in a positive frenzy of anticipation, hardly able to wait before taking off upriver.

When they start, Connemara white trout run hard. They need to, for the Connemara river knows a thing or two about stopping them. Most of these rivers are short, some with severe and sharp falls up which the white trout must struggle. A fall of say ten feet — and there are a number of these along the western coastal fisheries — is very difficult for a white trout to surmount and it needs a very big flood to enable him to do it. Running twenty or even thirty miles from the mouth of a fishery system right up to the feeder streams which form its uppermost limit is an onerous job for the white trout; small wonder then that it often takes him the whole summer to do it.

Good white trout rivers — that is, rivers which have plenty of white trout travelling up them — are primarily flood or spate rivers. White trout in general do not tarry in them. When moving up through a system during a flood, it is quite noticeable sometimes that if there is not enough water to carry them over the next obstacle or up into the next loch, they will fall back to the loch below. Several times, fishing a dropping system, have I seen white trout coming *back* down a river, going into reverse as it were. Kingsmill Moore confirms this when he writes "If the flood drops suddenly, they tail back to the lake they have last traversed." I would amend that to add that it is not necessarily a loch to which they drop back; if the river has a good holding pool with a slack current they will often stay there.

An over-view then of a typical western white trout fishery, one with stretches of swift and rocky rivers the best of which are non-alkaline connecting a series of lochs of varying sizes, would present a white trout behavioural pattern of great complexity. If there is enough water for them to do so, fish will be moving out of all the various lochs to run upriver to the next loch, other than the topmost ones, where they will stay mostly until ready for the final spawning run. But because some of the lochs retard the run-off of spate water, the lochs along an individual system will be affected in widely differing ways. In some there will be plenty of fresh water, in others much less, and sometimes in the bottom lochs hardly any at all. The running patterns of the white trout in all of these lochs will be similarly affected.

It is easy to understand then, how difficult it is for the white trout angler to hit it right. The ideal would be to have a rod on any one fisheryright throughout the fishing season — effectively from July to the middle of October — and to be on the right river and lochs every day, without exception, in all weather and water conditions. Even then, no really satisfactory or comprehensive overall picture of what was happening from one end of the fishery to the other would emerge — only a picture of what was happening wherever the angler happened to be. And even that would take care of just one fishery!

It is given to very few anglers — if any — to have that freedom. And so the average white trout angler either takes an hour or two from his work if he lives near his fishery or else relies on a week's holiday during the summer. His chances of striking it lucky are slim enough; but the great advantage of the Connemara fisheries in general is that the area's geographical structure favours the holding of water and thus gives a reasonable chance almost throughout the season for the angler.

For five years I lived in Connemara, within at the most an hour's drive of the best of its fisheries. In all that time, I rarely hit it right. All these fisheries are privately owned (except the Erriff which has now been taken over by the State and which is any case just outside the understood boundaries of Connemara) and rods on them generally have to be booked well ahead. I was dependent either on cancellations or vacant beats — not a satisfactory state of affairs but the best I could achieve and one which nonetheless enabled me to fish widely over Connemara and Mayo and — more importantly — to study at first hand the behaviour of the white trout in these western waters.

The sum of knowledge which those and other years have left me is absurdly small and amounts more to a series of don'ts than one of do's. Here for what they are worth are such convictions as these frustratingly difficult fish have left me with:

● In very warm water and weather, white trout are next to impossible to catch.

● A full and steady wind in otherwise settled weather is perhaps the best condition of all.

● White trout take best when they are freshly-run; equally white trout who have been loch-bound for some time and are "off the feed" will come back on it when heavy rain comes to raise the level and freshen the water.

● Barometric pressure is a vital factor in white trout fishing (and much more on this later).

● In calm conditions, small white trout or herling take better than big ones; in rougher water and weather the reverse seems to occur.

● If you have one of those days when every second cast brings a small brown trout, you will catch few white trout. I know not why (and more of this later too).

● White trout are unlike brown trout in that they are largely unmoved by hatches of natural fly. Kingsmill Moore puts this perfectly when he says "White trout have their time of 'taking', and if a rise of fly coincides with this time they will not overlook the natural, but a rise of natural will not necessarily bring them on the 'take'. The 'take' seems to be the result of a sudden burst of activity quite unrelated to food."

● There is a time of day when white trout move about, rather than remain in one position and it is more often than not from mid-morning to about lunchtime and then again in the late afternoon.

● The longer a white trout is in fresh water, the less likely it is to take a fly; but floodwater may easily change this.

● Fast-rising water, once the loch level has risen at all, is detrimental and seems to put the white trout off; thunder seems to have the same effect.

● Dry-fly is usually much inferior to wet-fly and white trout can be astonishingly clumsy when it comes to taking the dry-fly.

● When lying in lochs, white trout have distinct preferences for certain places. They like rocky, gravelly and sandy bottoms — there is a bay on the west side of Lough Inagh in Connemara which has a sandy bottom and which is a renowned lie for white trout, to take one instance; they also like shoals and reefs and outlying promontories. Above all they seem to haunt those places where shallows deepen and shelve. And in Connemara they prefer to take in water less than eight or nine feet deep.

● When white trout are moving in and around a time of high water, their movements are complex. If they are unsure as to whether there is enough water to carry them up a stretch of river from one loch to another, they will often congregate at that point where the river runs into the loch. Kingsmill Moore theorised that the white trout swim against the current to the mouth of the entering river and there rest, unwilling or unable to go any further. I think him right — and equally right when he supposed that white trout often populated the area around a river entrance before they dispersed around a loch, there to take up their favourite and time-honoured positions.

If there is an overall theme to all these points, it surely is that the white trout is a creature of very restrained and structured habits.

Chapter Eleven

Behaviour and Flies

Differences between brown and white trout — experiences on Lough Inagh — taking the fly — walkabout — tackle — flies — dislike of excess — some patterns — two great flies — the Bibio

The North bad, East worse, West good, but the South
Blows every bait into the Fish's mouth

George Smith, 1726

THE fundamental difference, literally, between brown and white trout feeding is that not alone do white trout feed far less in fresh water but their feeding habits are not related directly to food supply and its availability.

It has long been accepted that for practical purposes, salmon do not feed in fresh water. Certain it is that they do not feed for food purposes. White trout are not so extreme as that. They do feed but slightly. Small white trout or herling feed much more than adult and mature white trout but this does not alter the argument that the white trout is a poor and spasmodic feeder in fresh water.

The types of waters which the white trout favours, which are mostly acidic waters in poorly-sustained countryside, subject to frequent spates which disrupt and dislodge any invertebrate and plant life in them, are in any case badly-stocked larders for a hungry fish, which goes to explain why the brown trout in such rivers and lochs are small and undersized — and sometimes starving. But even this comparative dearth of food has little bearing on the pattern of white trout feeding in freshwater. They feed very little and there's an end on't.

It is often very hard for the brown trout angler to appreciate this. Accustomed to watching for and then matching the hatch, he finds his world turned awry. Like all who fish the fly for white trout, he must realise that by and large they do not generally take the fly in the belief that it is food but for some other reason, be it curiosity, playfulness, anger, fear or whatever. We do not know how fish feel;

but it is some feeling or feelings other than hunger which motivate a white trout, for most of the time anyway, to take an artificial fly.

I believe, very loosely, that there are two main ways or directions which we must follow to settle on where and when white trout take the fly. Certain it is that freshly-run fish, even when they are running (and despite F. W. Holiday's assertion that running fish are non-takers), are ready takers of the fly.

I give just one instance of many; last season, fishing the butts on Lough Inagh in Connemara with one of the finest white trout fishermen I know, we met a good run both of salmon and white trout running hard against a biggish current — it was a day after a heavy fall of rain. In half an hour he had four good white trout grassed; fishing above him and using the same tactic of wet-fly fished slowly across and down, I felt not a take. But I use this example not to point out the difference between an adequate white trout fisherman like myself and an exceptional one whose skill is instinctive but to show that white trout do take when running — at least in Ireland. And I have seen the same thing many times over.

Freshly-run white trout take well in lochs — providing you can find them. I have already dealt with where you might find them; the vital thing is to study the water conditions and figure out how these affect how and where the white trout is likely to run.

The second main way in which white trout take the fly is related to their daily habits. Anyone who has fished the Connemara lochs or those in Mayo will be mindful of the sharps and flats as it were of a day's fishing. Hours of idleness are punctuated by sudden action, soon followed by more idleness. An active morning can be followed by a dead afternoon. Rarely does a white trout loch fish well throughout a day, at least in the west of Ireland.

Close observation soon establishes a rough sort of pattern. There appear to be times during most days when white trout are conspicuously active and when they move about a loch, usually in shoals, but ranging quite widely from their normal lying spots. Mid-morning and late afternoon seem favoured times for this "walkabout" pattern. I am not suggesting that they do this every day in every loch at the same time. What I am saying is that in many of the lochs which I have fished there is a time when white trout seem to take better than at other times and that this seems to relate directly to an increase in their moving about a loch.

Most writers on white trout do not mention this habit, other than Kingsmill Moore. As with most of what he wrote about western Irish white trout fishing I find myself agreeing with him when he writes;

"the 'take' is, I believe, associated with the desire of the fish for a gentle constitutional. Certainly in calm weather the fish can be seen moving near the surface while the take is on." And amen and amen and amen to that!

As always, I sheer away from pontification or the dogmatic. But I do aver that all this reinforces a belief that far from being unpredictable, white trout are creatures of distinct habit. That these habits appear incomprehensible to us is no reason to deny that they exist. Exist they do — and the angler must accept and learn from them if he is to succeed.

Tackle for loch fishing

You can fish for white trout with brown trout tackle but you should bear in mind that you are not at all unlikely to hook an occasional salmon. Once on Lough Tawnyard in Mayo I broke my good white trout rod of split cane and turned to the only other rod I had in the car — an eight-foot glass fibre wand of such delicacy as to infer that its only suitable use would be to stir a cocktail. It stirred a salmon of some eight pounds who led me where he wished for an hour or so before I ran him ashore, still as fresh as a daisy and full of indignation at the trick I played on him. Such excitements are best avoided.

The rod — the ideal rod — is one of about ten to eleven feet. I prefer, a little regrettably, to use carbon or boron which can pick a longer line off the water than can a comparable split-cane rod. In a wind and wave white trout will take quite close to a boat but in finer, calmer weather they are difficult to approach. A rod which can cast a long line is then most useful.

The reel, other than the usual qualities, should be able to hold a full fly-line with at least 100 yards of backing, and preferably 150 yards. A big salmon might well need that and more.

Lines should of course, suit the recommended weight for the rod. I believe, for normal wet-fly work, that a slow-sinker is best. One of the best white trout anglers I know swears by his sink-tip, while another uses a floating line at all times. I find in calm conditions that an under-surface line causes less disturbance.

In certain conditions you may have to fish deep in search of white trout, in which case a spare reel with a heavy-sinking line is needed in your bag.

Nets should be capacious and rugged. They may have to land salmon as well as white trout. A two-foot diameter is not too much.

As with any form of loch or lake fishing, take plenty of rainproof and warm clothes. White trout waters lie in rainy country and you are certain at some stage to meet heavy rain while out in a boat.

Flies

The approach to choosing something close to a comprehensive list of
flies suitable for catching white trout is different from a similar one
for brown trout. It would not be too unfair to say, however, that
white trout flies have changed little over the years in comparison
with say, the expansion in design of brown trout flies. I would hazard
a guess that this is so because on the whole, white trout flies are non-
imitative patterns and that while it might be going too far to say that
almost anything will do, the angler does not need anything like so
wide a list as does the brown trout angler.

This of course has not stopped fly-tiers from producing a varied
range of white trout flies. Every Irish water has its own local flies —
the Delphi Silver, the Costelloe Blue and Silver for instance — and
all have their place. Yet from my own experience and those of other
white trout anglers whose wisdom I have respect for, a good angler
fishing with non-local flies will do as well as one fishing with local
ones. The great flies of white trout angling are, on the whole, great
wherever they are.

Firstly, size. I think most — or at least many — white trout anglers
use flies which are too big. To fish a size 8 fly at all times is ludicrous.
Far better to have a range of perhaps a couple of dozen patterns
(surely enough for anyone!) and to have those in three or even four
sizes, ranging up to size 12. Even in a high wind the recommended
changing to large patterns does not always work. Fishing Lough
Tawnyard, the top lake on the Erriff system in Mayo, I rose and
hooked fish after fish on a size 12 Connemara Black whilst my
companion, fishing a size 8, rose not a fish. Such fish as came to him
took a size 12 dropper (from memory a Claret and Mallard); my own
Claret, a size 12, also took fish. A switch to size 12s brought renewed
interest for my companion.

In general, white trout seem to dislike excess in flies. By that I
mean bright colours lavishly spread on a fly. There is often a distinct
difference between white trout flies as used in England (I am
thinking of Cumbria) and those of the west coast of Ireland. Irish
flies are subdued, clothed in sombre hue, full-bodied and even
straggly, as if they had not combed their hair or pressed their clothes
for some time — a far distance from the often slickly-dressed and
strutting Englishman. Is there an echo here of the sombreness of
western skies, dark rainclouds bundling over hills, the purple cloak
of peat? Perhaps; perhaps not; but certain it is that these rough-and-
ready lads of the west know and can do their job.

I would have most (but not all) of my white trout flies with a touch either of gold or silver, preferably in the rib; I would have my colours rich but subdued; and I would have them dressed not so far as to or around the bend as so many white trout flies seem to be these days. A good wide gape in the hook is useful — white trout have tender mouths, especially when freshly-run, and the wide gape allows a hook to gain a hold more easily.

As to a list of flies, my own includes Black Pennell, Connemara Black, Black and Silver, Claret and Mallard, Watson's Fancy, Kingsmill, Claret Bumble, Peter Ross, Butcher, Zulu, Bruiser, Bibio, Dunkeld. I always carry a few local flies for local waters but more from anxiety not to miss out than from a conviction that they are indispensable; they include the Delphi Silver, the Costelloe Blue and Silver, the Glenicmurrin Blue and a few others, including the Yellow Dyson which is good on some of the Mayo fisheries. As with brown trout, I am never without a copy of the Daddylonglegs. And for good measure, my white trout fly boxes contain several patterns more associated with brown trout but which catch the white too — Wickham, Invicta, Alexandra, Teal and Silver, Teal and Green etc. With all these, and perhaps a good sedge pattern or two, you will not be found wanting as far as fly patterns go.

I am aware that every other white trout angler will feel that I have left out some favourite flies from such a list. I am aware too, that these patterns are mostly traditional, other than the Kingsmills and the Bumbles, creations of Kingsmill Moore. In Northern Ireland, where my angling experience is limited, there are countless patterns of white trout flies from such marvellously inventive tiers as Hanna and M'Haffie; equally throughout the south, west and east coasts there are many, many individual patterns for white trout whose names rarely reach further than their local domains. I suspect that were anyone to compile a dictionary of Irish white trout flies it would be a thick volume — and what a splendid area for argument and debate it would make!

But I would point out, in defence of my choice, that these flies have served me well in a variety of Irish waters and that they include that particular range of hues (rather than colours) which white trout seem to favour — the clarets, blues and blacks which together with a little silver and/or gold, make up the greater part of the palette. If I were to be restricted to a choice of three flies those three colours would be there — the Connemara Black, the Claret and Mallard and the Bruiser the last choice of which many would quarrel with. But that is the way of it.

Kingsmill Moore, who put logic and practicality into his creative patterns, thought his Kingsmill greatly superior to the Connemara Black. I have not found it so, nor have I ever met a white trout angler in Ireland who thought it so either. The Connemara Black is a unique Irish fly and a uniquely successful catcher of Irish white trout. It is, with the Claret and Mallard, the most successful fly I have used for white trout. And I have tried most others.

A new dimension to white trout patterns is always possible. Hugh Falkus' range of surface lures is a case in point. I have tied some of them and found that while reasonably successful, they appear to demand such special conditions that their use is limited in ways in which the more traditional patterns are not. This is not to denigrate them; I think them excellent. But it is the way of life of most white trout anglers that they snatch their fishing when they can and must take such conditions as nature puts before them; all of that prevents them from much experimentation with new patterns, new ways of fishing. If you are staying a quick weekend in an angling hotel and dinner is at eight sharp, you are disinclined to take the evening off and fish the river with some fly you have never seen before. Of such laziness is convention established. And we are all to blame.

A much under-rated fly is the Bibio, in years past a stranger to the visiting angler but slowly establishing a solid reputation as a good taking fly for white trout not alone in Ireland but elsewhere. I believe the Bibio to be a Mayo fly, first tied by Major Roberts of the Burrishoole fishery in west Mayo, with its lovely lochs Furnace and Feeagh. Certainly it is an uncommonly good fly there, at home in the stark and stony hills of that beautiful county. But I am no historian of fly-tying.

In short-listing a selection of white trout flies it should be borne in mind that normal wet-fly methods demand the use of three flies. So some of the flies should have what anglers call a good "entry" — they should be sleek and slim to sink readily when used as tail flies on the leader tip. Others should be thick-bodied and fuzzy, like the Bumbles, Bruisers, Zulus etc., for use as droppers and to be dribbled along the surface. Never reverse the order. The old palmers of our fathers' day were primarily designed for use as droppers and very effective they were too. In reality any thick, fuzzy pattern, so long as it is dressed in the hues so favoured by white trout, will do its job as a dropper — and so long as its size meets with equal approval.

That question of size is another one to exercise the judgment of the angler. For white trout are choosy on that point. In general, and as a very rough rule-of-thumb, larger flies can be used in rough weather than during calmer conditions. On some Irish lochs a very big wave can rise, particularly when surrounding hills can channel and direct a wind down a loch with frightening velocity. Lough Inagh is such a loch. So too are Doolough and Glencullen on the Delphi fishery in Mayo, where the giant shoulder of Mweelrea pushes the wind tightly down the steeply-walled pass of Doolough, whipping the tops of the waves off in its anger.

Such weather does not necessarily prevent white trout from taking but it does make the use of larger flies than usual (say down even to sioze 8) desirable. Now and then you will get conditions which are unfishable; only last season (1982) I was blown off the tiny Lough Ashleam on the Screebe fishery in Connemara. Ashleam is scarcely more than a pond and at points you could cast a salmon fly right across its narrow width. But on this September day, despite a drogue, the boat drifted with such speed and the wind played havoc even with a single-fly leader that discretion won the day. Even so, a wayward fly found an eyelid and needed a doctor to remove the offending Black Pennell.

Even in that gale, however, Ashleam was fishing well with a run of biggish white trout several of which rose to and missed the fly. You could not keep a fly on the water before you over-ran it. Had the wind been ten miles an hour easier, great slaughter would have been done; but better a live angler than a dead one.

A magnificent east coast white trout of 10 pounds, 8 ounces, taken on fly from the River Boyne near Drogheda by Sir Richard Levinge. As a rule, white trout caught along the eastern and southern coasts are significantly bigger than those caught in the western fisheries of Connemara, Mayo and Donegal. As a counter-indicator, the record Irish white trout of 14lb 3oz was caught in County Mayo.

A small bag of Irish white trout showing clearly the small average size which is so characteristic of the west of Ireland fisheries, probably due to the poorer feeding off the coast. The white trout angler fishing in the west will find many fish weighing less than a pound, while a five-pounder calls for a round of Irish whiskies in the local pub.

Chapter Twelve

White Trout Tactics

Loch fishing — the drift — boat handling — dapping — salt water
fishing — my biggest white trout — the Irish record — river fishing
— timing — evening and night fishing — playing your trout

We care not who says,
And intends it dispraise,
That an angler to a fool is next neighbour:
Let him prate — what care we?
We're as honest as he;
And so let him take that for his labour.

Charles Cotton, 1670

I HAVE outlined already the three main ways in which white trout
are caught by fly-fishing in Ireland — loch, river and salt or
brackish/estuarine fishing. Of these the most consistent — and
consistently successful — is that of loch fishing.

River fishing by its nature is sporadic. White trout prefer acidic
and spate rivers and run up these only when there is enough water to
encourage them to do so. Even in a rainy country like Ireland, it is
surprising how infrequently the white trout meets such water
conditions as will enable him to run upriver unhindered; and thus
most river fishing in Ireland for white trout is a chancy business.,

In many areas, however, there are rivers with good holding pools
where the white trout can rest and wait for higher water and these
afford occasionally good fishing. But river fishing remains an uneven
business at best.

In many ways, saltwater fishing is difficult too. The angler is
dependent on tidal flow and its effects on the white trout. Saltwater
or brackish fishing needs special tackle — not many anglers will wish
to use their favoured Hardy rods or reels in salt water. Techniques
for fishing these waters with fly are thin on the ground amongst many
white trout men. And so the thrust of methods favours the loch.

Loch fishing

Boat or shore — or both? It is a question which detains some. Not me. For me it is a boat every time. You can cover almost all the water you want to fish and sometimes more than almost. And that will be more, much more, than you can do from a shoreline. Admittedly it is easier and safer to fish the shorelines of many white trout lochs than it is to fish brown trout lochs; the former lie usually in rocky areas and provide solid footing, whereas many brown trout lochs have hazardous shores. And shore fishing for white trout often provides the essential cover that you cannot get fully in a boat. There is too, the chance that in a high wind, shore casting may well be the only way to cover a particular area with a fly.

There are some differences between boat-angling for brown and white trout which need noting. White trout are far more nervous of a boat for one thing; and while all fish are alarmed by noise in a boat, such as tapping a pipe or noisily shifting a boot or dropping an oar, white trout are doubly so. It is very difficult indeed to approach white trout in a boat during calm conditions; and even when there is wind you must be cautious.

The traditional — and still most effective way — to fish for white trout from a boat is to drift. However you could fish the lochs of Connemara for years and not see anyone using either a drogue or an anchor. My thoughts on both I have already given in the chapter on lake trout and will not repeat here; suffice to say that the use of either or both helps a great deal when fishing for white trout.

The approach to the drift otherwise is also different. White trout shoal, unlike most brown trout and in any given drift it is quite possible that you will miss a shoal by a dozen yards and draw a complete blank, whereas the next parallel drift will bring you over the shoal — and suddenly you are into fish, possibly into several before you drift beyond the shoal.

Once you have determined where the holding areas are in any given loch, you must drift over them in a series of parallel drifts, leaving out none of the productive water. There is no point in carrying on a drift once you have passed over this water; instead row back (and I mean *row*, for outboard engines are anathema to white trout, although in big lochs I concede that they must be used) giving your next drift a wide berth so as not to alarm the fish. Take a bearing on some landmark before starting a new drift and take another one when you finish it; in that way you will be reasonably certain of fishing fresh water each time.

The position of sun and wind in a drift is something often

neglected. It stands to reason that if you drift with the sun behind you you are throwing a long shadow ahead of you. In shallow water especially this is alarming to the trout. If possible, avoid drifting with sun and wind at your back, remembering that as the position of the sun changes during the day a beat which was unfishable in the morning may well be fishable during the afternoon and vice versa (much the same often applies in river fishing).

By far the most satisfactory way to fish from a boat for white trout is to be on your own, with a knowledgeable and skilful ghillie at the oars. I stress those two adjectives, since ghillies vary widely on both counts. White trout lochs particularly demand a very close and intimate knowledge of underwater terrain and white trout lies and a ghillie needs to know them well. And he must handle a boat well — no splashing from the oars, no needless rowing, no extra manoeuvring and above all, he should be able to exercise an empathy with the angler's mind and method.

Such men are increasingly difficult to find. The expenses of running a white trout fishery in such a place as the west of Ireland have daunted many owners and in recent years there has been something of a rapid turnover in fishery ownership. Need I say that ghillies are the first casualty? Even in a land where employment of any sort is not easy to come by, young men seem curiously reluctant to row other people about for a living or part-living — that is young men who know something of what they are doing. For myself, had I the time, I can think of few more pleasurable occupations to while away a summer than ghillying.

Be that as it may, the real old Connemara ghillie, the man who knew each loch intimately is fast disappearing and the white trout angler will more often than not find himself left on his tod, and fending very much for himself. It behoves him, therefore, to be able to handle a boat well in conditions which are often tricky and sometimes downright dangerous, for many of these lochs are shallow and rocky and it is a very simple thing indeed to tip a boat over on a reef in a wind.

Most of the boats on the white trout lochs are smaller than the big Corrib boats which at 18 feet long, have the beam to go with it and are much better in a big sea than some of the slimmer 16 and 17-footers which you will find increasingly on white trout lochs. It is very difficult for three people to fish from anything under 21 feet; in a 17 or 18-foot boat, two skilled anglers can fly-fish, one from each end, and the man in the middle, angler or ghillie, can dap. But it is better for one man to devote his whole time and attention to handling a boat, especially if there is anything of a wave running.

Boat handling is vital to success in white trout fishing on lochs. As I have said, drifting must be parallel, should be only over the good spots and must not waste a square foot of good water, nor waste time fishing water which is non-holding. The wind direction may not necessarily permit a boat to drift naturally along the desired drift path, in which case the boatman will have to manoeuvre the boat with his oars downwind, sometimes across wind and sometimes indeed even upwind and across. That all this needs real skill and judgment at the oars goes without saying.

The traditional methods of drift fishing — allowing the boat to drift before the wind and casting straight out in front of the boat as it drifts along — do work. But I feel very strongly that they are limiting. The straight, forward cast is an easy way out, allowing the anglers not to worry too much about catching each other rather than the fish. Crosswind casting, and working the flies back across or diagonally through the waves rather than at right angles is a far more effective way to cover water than the normal method. The fact that it needs co-ordination and timing if both anglers — or even one — are to use it need not mean its demise. By casting in rotation rather than together, and by varying the direction and length of cast intelligently, two sensible anglers using the crosswind method will cover twice the water or more that normal straight casting would cover.

The length of cast too, is important. Remember that white trout are more wary of a boat than brown trout, especially in calm water. I cast further for white trout, although there is no real need of this in a good wave.

How many flies? Three is normal and that number has evolved after the supporting proof of many decades as to its efficacy. If you can fish three flies, by all means do so, although there will be times in flat calms when one fly is enough. Three flies allow you a variety — a tail fly with a good entry, a middle dropper which may be the same pattern as the tail but of a smaller or larger size and a good bushy top dropper. A long rod allows the top dropper to be used properly — when the retrieve is nearly finished, the dropper should be allowed to bobble on the surface, when white trout often take with tremendous *élan* (or at least try to, since their aim at the bobbling dropper is often awry).

Vary the retrieve, from fast to slow, from smooth to intermittent; a trial will show which works best. I find a smooth and level retrieve is best. If no fish are moving, there is no point in both rods persisting with that method which has been unsuccessful. Use a deep-sinking line and some good big lures and get down to the fish, while the other rod can keep on with shallow wet-fly tactics. In calm conditions, a dry-fly line is best; grease the leader to within two feet or so of the fly, using a single fly only, and work it quietly and gently back. If white trout are rising, as they will do in a calm sometimes, cover the rises.

Be adaptable. If by mid-day there is no action at all, desperate measures are called for. Use every method until you get the fish to move. If all fail, at least you have tried. It is surprising how a change of tactics sometimes works; I have even dapped a dry daddy imitation and taken fish. I am often caught out this way, especially when I have fished all day without a decent rise and suddenly an enormous white trout has an electric slash at the fly out of the blue. Last year, once on Shindilla on the Screebe system and once on Tawnyard on the Erriff, I missed two tremendous white trout at the heel of two otherwise almost blank days. It is so easy to lose your concentration.

Dapping is always worth trying. There is no doubt at all that the biggest white trout go for the daddylonglegs dapped in windy conditions and I would guess that by far the greatest proportion of white trout over three or four pounds in Connemara are caught on the dap. It can be a wearisome business but at its best it is unbearably exciting and always worth a try if there is wind enough and if other methods have failed. It also allows a boatman to fish. Never deride the dap; it is so often the saviour of the loch angler.

Saltwater fishing

My early white trout fishing was done in saltwater, on an incoming tide using sandeels for bait. And very good it was too. But bait-fishing is outside the scope of this book.

It is perfectly possible to catch white trout on the fly in saltwater. In fact there are times when it is the only way in which you will catch them, especially during those periods of dry summer in late July and August when there is not enough fresh water to move them.

While the techniques of fly-fishing in saltwater are really little different from those used in freshwater, the timing is everything. You may well catch white trout at times other than the incoming tide but they are few. White trout which feed offshore move into the mouths of rivers when the tide begins to flood; and they feed over the shore covered by the flooding tide and then drop back again on the ebb tide, providing of course that they do not run up the river.

My saltwater fly-fishing is limited largely for two reasons — one, that these days my white trout fishing is restricted largely to the western lochs and two, that I prefer fishing in freshwater. It is difficult enough to find suitable conditions for loch fishing; but to be restricted to tidal times is even more prohibitive. If I had the time to spend a month or so doing nothing else but fishing in saltwater it is entirely possible that this attitude might change. But it remains an activity quite rarely indulged in.

Hugh Falkus has so comprehensively covered every aspect of saltwater fishing that there is little room for anyone else, other than to describe my own methods, which have the advantage of having worked for me.

If I can — and if I have the time — I make a low-water survey of the area I am about to fish, noting good pools and possible feeding areas, rocks, snags, configuration of channel and outlying banks and shoals — in other words, I get a good grasp of the topography which once the tide comes in, will of course be invisible under its blanket of water.

It is very important to choose a spot from which, once you begin fishing, you will be able to cover feeding fish. Such a spot must have other attributes, such as allowing you a line of retreat once the water gets too high for you to wade in safety; the surroundings should not be too weedy, or prevent you from casting in a reasonably wide range around you and the current should not be such as to sweep you off your feet or cause you difficulty in operating freely.

White trout moving in at the mouth of a river at the flooding tide seem to feed well. I would not like to be more positive. But they do feed, most freely along the edges of banks of weed which of course shelter many small animals and other forms of food. Remember that at certain times of the flooding tide the effects of the seaward current of the river will be greatly lessened and that this will encourage white trout to move all over the river instead of keeping to well-defined paths of upriver movement. Remember too that many animals — sandeels, rag-worm, lugworm, mussels, clams, limpets and dozens more — feed once they are covered by water. And if they are active, the white trout will be equally so.

The actual angling technique is simple. Loch tackle will do, except that it should be reserved especially for saltwater use — no one likes to ruin a good cane rod or an expensive reel and fly-line through saltwater effects. I use a heavyish glass rod of about ten feet, an old sinking trout line, a leader of about ten feet but with a 9 lb. tip (very often you will have to manhandle heavy white trout in weedy water) and big flies. I think that fly pattern is unimportant. What is important is size and coloration of fly, the two blended so that they resemble some form of food which the white trout is after.

This primarily means lure fishing. The pattern of lure, once it conforms to the rough picture outlined above, is largely immaterial. I quite frequently (comparatively speaking) use low-water salmon flies, very lightly-dressed and with plenty of silver; I have tied some of Falkus' lures and found them first-class. If you are a fly-tier it is the simplest thing in the world to tie a white trout lure for saltwater fishing. But use a single hook — doubles are heavy and weigh down the end of a fly, causing it to behave unnaturally in the water. The vital thing is to get the fly or lure working well in the trout's taking area, which may well mean getting it right down to the bottom where the trout are feeding on molluscs and worms and occasionally sandeels which they appear to like almost better than anything else.

My best white trout was caught on fly in saltwater. I will not reveal the river other than to say loosely that it was in the south-west of Ireland. Earlier in the day I had taken a good look at the location, below a stone bridge where a small-sized but deep river ran a short length out into the sea through dense banks of weed. That evening after tea I stationed myself on a little reef or group of rocks on the seaward side of the bridge and opposite a deepish pool. I was using freshwater loch flies, as I had none others with me at the time; a Butcher on the tail and a big Peter Ross higher up.

As the tide flooded in and the water ran its muddied fingers up through the weedbeds and dried-out rocks, I began to fish. There was no sign of a feeding fish; but at about mid-tide, having fished for nearly an hour, I hooked and lost what seemed a goodish fish. Five minutes later I hooked another who ran seaward, jumped twice in quick skittering succession and threw the fly. It was getting dark when I hooked a third fish who played heavily in the deep pool and who tried everything to bury himself in the weed. But after a good fight he came to the net — just over three pounds.

By this time, though it was quite dark. I could hear very clearly the white trout feeding. Several times a big back showed on the surface and once I thought I saw a salmon. Two more fish fell to me, each about a pound. And then suddenly the fishing eased off. A couple of last casts — and then there was a sudden wrenching take that almost dragged me off balance and into the by-now deep water.

I do not know how I managed to keep that fish on the hook. It was dark as black ink (my biggest fish have all, significantly enough, been caught in the dark) and between trying to keep my balance and attempting to give this fish no quarter at all, I was confused — so

confused and so unable to see what was going on that I did not know
for much of the fight where the fish was.

For a time he bored upriver; then he turned and ran back
downriver while I, realising too late that he had done so, tried
desperately to recover slack line. When he jumped again I thought
he was gone; but then he came up near my feet and cruised up and
down, sending down through the rod that unyielding solidity of feel
and power which only big fish have.

It was at this stage that I began to realise that I might yet land
him. I kept on strong sideways pressure, trying to turn his head and
tire him (a fish who gets his head down directly beneath the angler,
such as when boat-fishing, is far more difficult to pressurise than
when using side pressure); and in a few minutes he came to the
surface and splashed tiredly once or twice. Another slight run and
bore and he came again to the top, where I could see the faint whitish
splash he made. I reached for the net, which I had stuck handle-
down in a cleft between two rocks beside me. It was not there.
Whether I had knocked it over, whether the water had swept it away,
it had gone.

By now rain was falling heavily and a wind had begun to get up. I
felt very clearly the perils of my position; I was about twenty yards
from shore and although the ridge of rocks on whose seaward
extremity I now stood extended right in to the shore, I was so unable
to make out any landmarks that I was very unsure of where the ridge
actually lay. Feeling carefully with my feet, I moved sideways
towards the shore, keeping a gingerly-tight hold on the fish; gently I
towed him behind me, the while literally sweating with a mixture of
anxiety and fear.

Then I was ashore and the belt of trees above the tideline loomed
out of the darkness. Very carefully I drew the fish, by now on his side,
up the shelving beach; and then I fell on him. By the light of my little
pocket torch, whose battery was so low that it shed light no further
than a few feet, he scaled six and a half pounds on my scales. And
that is my biggest white trout.

I never recovered my net. The next morning I went back but it had
vanished. I cared not. It had been worth the loss of a net just for that
one big fish.

The record Irish white trout, one of 14 lb. 3 oz., was caught in
saltwater — but on bait. Its captor, Dr. Eoin Bresnihan, himself a
keen fly-fisherman and an habituée of the Connemara white trout
lochs together with that finest of white trout anglers, Harry Hodgson
of Currarevagh, thought it a salmon after he had caught it on the

beach in Achill Island in County Mayo and celebrated this unusual capture in the local pub. Whether or not the good Irish whiskey caused a re-think or not is debatable; but a proper analysis showed it later to be a white trout. A noble fish indeed — and what would I give to hook it on light fly tackle! And I wonder how many such big white trout are mistakenly credited as being salmon?

Saltwater fly-fishing is a specialised area of white trout fishing and there is no doubt in my mind that in Ireland it is neglected and infrequently practised. It is an essential accessory in the angler's armoury and has the priceless benefit of producing more good fish than almost any other method, besides offering the angler the chance to catch the fresh and feeding fish.

River fishing

In most areas where white trout run in Ireland, river fishing is confined to those times of spate, or when the rivers are high enough for white trout to run up them, or in the evenings.

Spate fishing is rarely good fly-fishing. Spate rivers can and do become highly coloured in anything like a flood and it is very hard for white trout or any other fish in those conditions even to see a fly at close range. During spates worming when the river is dropping slightly is much better — but outside the scope of this book.

In certain and very specific conditions, white trout will take a fly when the river is running high. I have had several good days on some south-eastern rivers when the water has fined down to a sherry colour, for instance. In such cases all my fish were caught between eight and ten miles from the river mouth and all these fish were of that bright silver colour that denotes a freshly-run fish. The inference is that these fish had run upriver during the spate and were either continuing upriver under the impetus of heightened water or had otherwise paused to rest, being still, however, inclined to feed. All were caught two to three days after the heaviest of the spate. The fact that these very definitely fresh fish had run eight to ten miles in heavy water in two to three days speaks eloquently of the energy and running power of the white trout.

I do not really like fishing in spate conditions or even after the water has fined down somewhat but is still running heavily coloured. I have never been able to define this dislike, other than to suggest, if hesitantly, that I feel I am taking unfair advantage of the white trout and also that there is a great element of luck in such fishing.

I believe from watching them that white trout run deep in heavy waters for I have rarely seen them moving other than forcing their way over shallows or ascending falls. Thus deep-fishing tactics are called-for. And I dislike such tactics, not from any moral reaction but because I find them less pleasurable to use. After all, I argue to myself, much of the pleasure in fishing stems from how you fish, from the feel of the tackle in your hands, from watching the floating fly or the semi-submerged one. Deep tactics — and often they yield more fish than others — are not total anathema to me; but I find other ways more enjoyable and that is why I pursue them.

Daytime river fishing for white trout is, as I have said, mostly confined to rivers in a falling spate or to those which have enough water for white trout to run upriver. There are, however, rivers in such places as Donegal and Kerry which have splendid holding pools where white trout rest, awaiting high water before moving on. White trout rest in the stillest water they can find in a river but it must be water which is well-oxygenated — a fact which is often forgotten by anglers.

The value of a well-oxygenated pool is incalculable and the angler must be able to distinguish between one which is and one which is not. When resting in a river, white trout have a distinct preference for the slowest of water, harbouring their strength both for the final run upriver to spawn and the act of spawning itself in the late autumn. But they are not easy to catch even when the water is fresh with rain. As a general rule, the lower the water, the more reluctant they are to take; and in a fine and dry spell, with low water and every holding pool packed with white trout, he is a good man who catches one of any size, although the smaller trout will often take in conditions which put off their elders.

As with every aspect of white trout angling, the timing on a river is everything. When the water is falling, and has fallen so that while there is still colour in it, it is time to try a favoured tactic — the use of upstream wet-flies. Very few anglers indeed pursue this method for white trout but during that time when the water has fallen so as to make the use of standard-sized white trout flies a useless exercise (as with brown trout, Irish anglers use flies which are too big for much of their fishing time), small flies fished wet and upstream can do considerable damage to the white trout population. Again it is a question of getting the timing perfect — the water must be right, the day must be right (neither too much sun or too much wind).

Evening fishing on rivers is a much more stable exercise and can be very good indeed. Few people in Ireland fish at night — that is after eleven o'clock at night through to dawn the next day; I have done so a few times but while I have caught fish, it is both personally inconvenient and often impossible, the demands of having to work in the morning or escort a family during holiday, overcoming such slight desire as I have to fish on through the night. But evening fishing is convenient and often efficacious.

Basically this sort of fishing demands simple tactics. You can for once use largish flies and the white trout do not seem greatly concerned about patterns. I have used many but the successful ones have all had several characteristics in common — they have been bushy and quite heavily dressed. It is no harm at all if the fly drags. The flight of the sun (which white trout seem to dislike) and the cool of evening appear to help to stir the fish; whatever the reasons (and I am sure they are many) the fact remains that white trout in a river are on the *qui vive* much more in the evening than during the day.

During this time your tactics will depend on a variety of factors. If the water is high and fish are clearly in a mood to take, downstream and across is as good as any. But when white trout are waiting in a holding pool and take their evening promenade, to fish for them downstream is disastrous. Far better to approach them in the manner of fishing the evening rise for brown trout; and although the fly need not be fished dry, these are trout with an eye on the surface so fish for them at that level.

A point to remember — and one forgotten by many brown trout men who have an occasional stab at the white trout — is that white trout shoal. If you disturb a shoal either by catching, pricking or alarming fish, your chances of extracting further trout from the shoal are gone. By fishing from below with small wet-flies, you can work your way through much of a shoal.

Such methods make other demands. You should never, when trying to net a fish, allow it to run downstream so much so that you have to drag it upstream to your net. You are almost bound to lose it, especially in any sort of current. On the other hand, you cannot allow a hooked fish to run upriver to disturb the other fish in the pool. With a big fish, there isn't much you can do anyway; but try to put pressure on such fish to run downriver rather than up and then follow them, playing them so that when you come to net them, you do so from downstream of the fish. Bankside growth, outcropping rocks, steep banks — all these and other hazards may prevent you from following big fish downriver. But you must do your best.

Much more so than with brown trout, white trout angling depends very much on the angler's timing in getting to the water at the right time, when wind, water and other weather conditions are right. That is demanding a great deal, especially from those anglers who live far from a good white trout water and whose white trout angling is confined to times of holidays or quick breaks for a weekend or whatever. Small wonder then that many anglers forswear the white trout forever, after weeks, months and sometimes even years without hitting on the right conditions.

Even so, the careful and thoughtful angler can take fish in conditions which are far from ideal. If the weather is at all settled, and the waters are not too low, then there is always a chance. And this slender, silver fish, whose fight is so splendidly frenetic and abandoned, is worth taking such a chance for.

Fishing the butts on the Burrishoole fishery in County Mayo — a favoured spot when white trout are running. They take a fly well fished in the slightly slower water, where the fly is allowed to work itself wholly naturally. Burrishoole is one of the finest of the western fisheries.

Appendix I

The Principal Brown Trout Lakes in Ireland

The waters listed here are those which to my knowledge and in my experience offer the angler the best chance of finding some reasonably good trout fishing. It is no accident that on nearly all of them, the Inland Fisheries Trust (now the Central Fisheries Board) has had a significant input towards developing the angling.

It is no accident either that of all the large lakes listed, every single one lies wholly or partly over a limestone bed, giving rich feeding. Anglers can expect trout on these bigger lakes to be on average bigger than those in the smaller lakes.

Some of the waters are free, such as the great western lakes, while others are either locally preserved or require anglers who fish them to be members of the Central Fisheries Board. If you are not a member of a local angling club, the CFB or have not received permission from riparian owners to fish, it is up to you to do so in most cases.

It is possible to hire boats on most if not all of the lakes listed here. It is outside the scope of this book to advise on where boats can be obtained but local inquiry in towns, villages, angling centres, tackle shops, hotels and guesthouses usually will elicit the relevant information.

Central Fishery Board lakes, where the CFB has sole control, are very cheap to fish at £3 a day for the boat alone. On the bigger lakes, charges vary greatly and you can pay up to £30 a day for a boat, engine and ghillie — all three a prerequisite if you are fishing say, Mask or Corrib and don't know the lake. This however, is the highest price I have ever been quoted and you should not have to pay that much.

Large lakes
Lough Arrow, County Roscommon
Lough Carra, County Mayo

Lough Conn, County Mayo
Lough Corrib, County Galway
Lough Cullin, County Mayo
Lough Derravaragh, County Westmeath
Lough Ennell, County Westmeath
Lough Inchiquin, County Clare
Lough Mask, County Mayo
Lough Melvin, County Sligo
Lough Owel, County Westmeath
Lough Sheelin, County Cavan

   A word of caution. Lough Ennell in Westmeath is recovering from severe pollution and at the time of writing, the Central Fisheries Board has requested members to allow Ennell's trout time to recover also. Lough Sheelin, also touching on Westmeath but principally a Cavan lake, is struggling to stay alive. Large areas of Lough Melvin lie in Northern Ireland, where there are stricter legal requirements to be met by anglers.
   The list of smaller lakes (below) is highly subjective. Some anglers will wonder why certain small lakes have been left out. In defence, I would say that those listed are reasonably certain to provide good fishing, given suitable weather and water conditions. Again they should not be fished without first ascertaining who owns the fishing rights; in many cases, but not all, these belong to the CFB.

Smaller lakes
Lough Acalla, County Galway (rainbows)
Lough Annagh, County Cavan (also holds rainbows)
Ballyline, County Clare
Ballyteigue, County Clare
Bilberry Lough, County Mayo
Dromore, County Clare
Lough Emly, County Monaghan
Lough Gill, County Sligo
Lough Glore, County Westmeath
Gortglass Lake, County Clare
Lough Leane, County Kerry
Lough na Leibe, County Sligo (rainbows)
Lough O'Flynn, County Roscommon
Pallas Lake, County Offaly (also holds rainbows)
Raha Lake, County Clare
Lough Rea, County Galway

Shepperton Lakes, County Cork (also hold rainbows)
White Lake, County Westmeath (also holds rainbows)

Northern Ireland trout lakes

Fishing in Northern Ireland is much more strictly controlled than in the Republic. Trout anglers must have rod licences, and in some cases fishing permits also. Northern Ireland's trout fishing is best divided into two parts, one where fishing is controlled by the Foyle Fisheries Commission based in Derry, the other by the Fisheries Conservancy Board for Northern Ireland, based in Portadown, County Armagh. In addition, many waters are supervised by the Department of Agriculture, which requires anglers to have a permit to fish its waters.

If angling in the North generally costs more than in the Republic, it is much more carefully run, an easier task with much smaller trout waters than in the south. In many cases, fly fishing only is allowed. It would be fair to say however, that angling pressure, particularly on those lakes and reservoirs close to cities and towns, is greater in the North than in the Republic.

Brown and rainbow trout lakes

Achork, County Fermanagh
Aughnagurgan, County Armagh
Bantry, County Tyrone
Bellanaleck Lake, County Fermanagh
Bradan Reservoir, County Tyrone
Castlewellan Lakes, County Down
Coolyermer, County Fermanagh
Corrann, County Fermanagh (rainbows)
Corry, County Fermanagh
Craigavon Lakes, County Armagh
Darkly, County Armagh (rainbows)
Dungonnel Reservoir, County Antrim
Lower Lough Erne, County Fermanagh
Gentle Owens, County Armagh
Glencreavan, County Fermanagh
Keenaghan, County Fermanagh
Killylane Reservoir, County Antrim
Leathemstown Reservoir, County Antrim
Loughbrickland, County Down
Lough Melvin, County Fermanagh
Meenameen, County Fermanagh

Mountfield Lakes, County Tyrone
Roughan Lough, County Tyrone (rainbows)
Shaw's Lake Reservoir, County Armagh
Stoneyford Reservoir, County Antrim
Tullynawood, County Armagh (rainbows)
Woodburn Reservoir, County Antrim

Appendix II

The Principal Brown Trout Rivers in Ireland

Any list of trout rivers anywhere must necessarily be selective and subjective. In the Republic, trout rivers face so many problems, day-in and day-out, that the miracle is that so many of them still hold fish.

Apart from regular and sporadic pollution, which mostly comes either from industrial or agricultural waste entering a river and or its feeders, and also from town sewage, Irish rivers have many other dangers hovering above them. Water extraction so far has largely been confined to large lakes but is nonetheless a serious, if hidden danger in that lower lake levels mean lower river levels downstream.

But by far the most consistent wrecker of rivers has been drainage work. Many of the river systems mentioned below have been drained; and while some have recovered partially, none are nearly as good as they once were.

Visiting anglers, therefore, should always check with the local regional fishery board, angling clubs, tackle shops etc. as to the quality of the water they propose to fish.

Principal trout river systems
Liffey — flows through Wicklow, Kildare and Dublin. Middle reach is excellent — a typical limestone stream with appropriate fly-life. Heavily fished and nearly all club water. Best tributary is the King's River, which holds mostly small trout.

Boyne — wrecked by drainage a decade ago, the Boyne is recovering. It runs from Offaly through Meath and is a superb piece of limestone water, with big fly hatches and heavy trout. Best fishing is around Trim, where the river has best recovered. Good tributaries are the Stoneyford, Deel, Trimblestown and both Kells Blackwater and south Meath Blackwater. Best fishing is club or private.

Slaney — flows through Wicklow, Carlow and Wexford. Mostly stony, non-limestone water, with occasional limestone stretches.

Excellent trout fishing for smallish fish. Most of the good water is club-controlled or in private hands. Useful tributaries are the Bann and Boro.

Barrow — big limestone river flowing through the peat-and-limestone midlands from Laois through Kildare, Carlow and Waterford. Fishing very localised and occasionally polluted. Splendid trout fishing, best between Carlow and St. Mullins. Best tributaries are Slate and Figile south of Edenderry, the Bog River near Athy and the Greese, Graney and Lerr. The best water is club-controlled or in private hands.

Nore — biggish, fastish river, mostly stony, running from the hills in Offaly through Kilkenny to join the Barrow in Co. Carlow. Better trout water than is generally held, though fish are small.
    The best of the Nore angling is below Kilkenny. Mostly club-controlled or in private hands. The Nore's best tributaries (which are claimed to be better than the big river itself) are the King's River, near Callan; the White Horse River near Mountrath; the Dinan near Castlecomer; and the Gayle and Erkina near Durrow.

Suir — a truly magnificent, but polluted limestone river, big and handsome which confines itself mostly to Tipperary. Lord Grey of Fallodon thought it better than the Test or Itchen. Typical limestone water with plenty of good trout, and so many good stretches that there is no room to list them. All the best water is club or private. The best tributaries are the Annagh, Clodiagh, Aherlow, Tar and Multeen, while the swift Neir is also said to be useful.

Blackwater — primarily a salmon, roach and dace water but with good trout fishing. Rises in Kerry and flows through Cork and Waterford. Middle reaches running over sandstone are probably best and all the good water is club or private. The best tributaries, probably better than the main river, are the Bride and Funcheon, though the latter has been destroyed several times by wanton pollution. The Awbeg is also useful.

Lee — like the Blackwater, mostly a sandstone river, flowing through Cork. Excellent fishing but smallish fish. Some free water. Best tributaries are the Laney and the Sullance.

Shannon — the best thing about Shannon trout fishing is its tributaries — the main river, the longest in either Britain or Ireland, scarcely being a trout river at all. The best tributaries are the Big Brosna, which runs from Westmeath through Offaly to join the Shannon at Lough Ree, and is a typical midland limestone stream, with some excellent fishing (CFB controlled); the Mulcaire, which flows through Limerick to join the Shannon above Limerick city, another good limestone stream; the Nenagh River, again limestone and flowing through Tipperary to join the Shannon at Lough Derg; Little Brosna (CFB) flowing through Offaly to Lough Derg; the Inny, flowing all the way from Cavan to Lough Ree, and offering patchy fishing; and the Clodiagh and Silver Rivers, tributaries in turn of the Big Brosna. All these rivers are limestone streams which have been drained; the fishing, if patchy and localised, is often first-class and mostly dry-fly water.

Another useful Shannon tributary is the Suck in Roscommon and Galway and it itself has several excellent tributaries, the best of them being the Bunowen (said by those who should know to offer the best river angling in Europe but far from that in my experience), and the Shiven.

Smaller rivers

Wicklow rivers — all mostly mountainy, rocky rivers with small trout and so can be taken together. Best are the Avoca, Dartry, Dargle, Inch and Owenavarragh (the latter once was a most useful white trout stream, as I well recall). Some free water but mostly club.

Bandon — flows through Cork. A river which always looks as though it should fish better than it does. Fast and stony, there is good fishing here and there. Mostly club or private.

Laune — purely a Kerry river and can be excellent. Looks like a limestone river but is not. Good dry-fly stretches, and mostly club or private water.

Deel — flows through Limerick and is trying to recover from drainage. Was an excellent trout stream but very patchy now. Much the same thing can be said about its cousin, the Maigue. Good fishing here and there but very localised. Mostly club or private water.

Fergus — a splendid limestone river in Clare, with the best of the water around Ennis. Subject to low water during summer due to porous limestone. Mostly club or private fishing.

Claregalway — recovering from drainage (which in places has left steep rocky cliffs twenty feet high and inaccessible for anglers), this once-splendid limestone stream flows through Galway. Like its near-neighbour the Black River, it has sporadically good trout fishing. Mostly free water.

Robe — a tributary of Lough Mask, flows through Mayo and is now being drained. Bombarded by Ballinrobe sewage, it has had a tough time but can be a very good trout river. Not recommended for the next decade.

Moy — primarily a Mayo salmon river but that it holds good brown trout is not generally known — the best water is in the upper limestone reaches.

Garavogue — flows through Sligo; good limestone water and occasionally excellent fishing. Club and private water.

Other waters — there are literally hundreds of small rivers around Ireland, many of them giving localised but good fishing. Local inquiries are always best for this sort of thing.

Appendix III

The Principal White Trout Fisheries in Ireland

Almost without exception, the best white trout fishing in the Republic is along the western seaboard, running from Kerry in the south-west corner all the way northwards past Clare, Galway, Mayo, Sligo and Donegal.

The best of the country's white trout fishing is preserved to a greater or lesser degree. The best fisheries are usually in most demand and it is often difficult, if not impossible, for a visiting angler to get a rod on one of them during the height of the season and more especially when water conditions are right.

The following list includes all of the well-known fisheries and some which are not so well-known. Anglers who wish to fish them should telephone or write to the relevant fishery long in advance. Boats can be hired on most — but certainly not all — of the fisheries, many of which do not allow outboard engines, particularly on some of the often-tiny Connemara lochs. As a rough rule, a boat without engine or ghillie will cost about £6 to £8 a day; an engine is an extra £5 a day (usually with petrol extra). Boat, engine and ghillie will cost a minimum of £22 a day and often more. River fishing is allocated by beat and can vary from one to three or four rods or even more per beat. As prices vary so much, anglers are advised to contact the fishery they select and to inquire about costs and facilities.

Principal Fisheries (Co. Kerry)
Lough Currane — in Waterville in Kerry is arguably the finest white trout lake in the Republic. The whole of the lake and a short piece of the river are free. You need a boatman to fish Currane, as the white trout have defined lies which only the old hand knows. Most of the rivers which flow into Currane are preserved by the various hotels in the area.

Caragh — like Currane, both river and lake. Excellent white trout but preserved mostly by local hotels.

121

Laune — flows out of Killarney into Dingle Bay. Has fairish runs of white trout. Mostly club and private water, though some bits are free.

Feale — runs through north Kerry into the Shannon. Can be very good but is signally liable to pollution. I once saw several thousand white trout killed near Listowel by wanton discharge of pollution into the Feale. Mostly club or private water.

Co. Galway (including Connemara)

Crumlin — near Spiddal, west of Galway. Several lakes and a short river. Preserved.

Cashla — one of the finest in Connemara. In two sections — the lower Costello, including several lakes and the Cashla River, and the upper Costello, which includes Fermoyle, Clogher and Shanawora, and the Fermoyle River. Preserved and sometimes difficult to get a rod on.

Screebe — a marvellous fishery in its day. Plenty of lakes from Shindilla down, and some excellent river pods. Preserved.

Lettermucknoo — a series of lakes but not so noted as its near neighbour Screebe. Preserved.

Furnace — not to be confused with the lake of the similar name in Mayo. Again a series of lakes near Screebe. Preserved.

Inver — two chains of lakes near Kilkieran. One of the better fisheries. Preserved.

Carna — another chain of lakes draioning into Bertraghboy Bay. Preserved.

Gowla — chain of lakes and a goodish river, draining into Bertraghboy Bay. An excellent fishery. Preserved.

Ballynahinch — perhaps the single most important white trout fishery in Connemara, including river and lake. Preserved.

Doohulla — several lakes and a small river draining into Ballyconneely Bay. Preserved.

Inagh and Derryclare — Inagh is one of the premier Connemara white trout lakes and the river connecting it with Derryclare a famous spot for a white trout. Excellent fishery but needs local knowledge on a biggish lake. Preserved.

Kylemore Abbey — three lakes near the so-called abbey, which is really a school. Excellent fishery. Preserved. Includes the heavily-poached Dawros River and the Culfin River.

Kylemore House Fishery — three lakes. Preserved.

Top waters, Ballynahinch — not to be confused with the more famous main Ballynahinch fishery. Five lakes and a good fishery. Preserved.

Co. Mayo

Erriff — includes the famous river, now state-owned, and the separate and entrancing Tawnyard lake, which is itself a splendid fishery. Both preserved.

Delphi — beloved of Kingsmill Moore, three lakes drained by the Dundorragha into Killary Harbour. Excellent fishery but like the Erriff, vulnerable to poaching at the narrow inlet into Killary. Preserved.

Carrowniskey — a couple of lochs and a longish river, this is not heavily fished and can be first-class. Preserved.

Newport — really two fisheries; the Newport House fishery includes the splendid Newport river fishing and half of Lough Beltra at the top end, the other half being run by the Glenisland Co-Op Society. Both river and lake are first-class. Preserved.

Burrishoole — owned by the state, home of the Bibio fly, and a first-class white trout fishery which includes the two lakes Feeagh and Furnace. Preserved.

Owenmore — good white trout river, much dependent on water conditions. Preserved.

Owenduff — very similar to the Owenmore.

Co. Sligo
Easkey — heavily-fished but good river fishery. Preserved.

Ballisodare — the best parts of this excellent river fishery are family-owned and rarely see a visiting angler. Preserved. More of a salmon river.

Co. Donegal
Bundrowes — really not a Donegal river but it does end at Bundoran in that lovely county. Flowing out of Lough Melvin, it has some good white trout and is preserved.

Owenea — excellent river fishery, with plenty of tributaries along its 16 miles. Preserved.

Note: Besides the fisheries listed here, there are literally hundreds of small rivers and streams around Ireland which hold white trout. Some are better than others. Inquire locally.

Appendix IV

Laws, Licences and Tackle Dealers

Brown and Rainbow Trout

No licence is required to fish for brown and/or rainbow trout in the Republic of Ireland.

In Northern Ireland, trout anglers must have a rod licence and in some cases, fishing permits also. Those waters which are controlled by the Northern Ireland Department of Agriculture can only be fished under permit.

In the Republic, while no licence is required other than for white trout and salmon, all those waters controlled by the Central Fisheries Board require a permit. Anglers wanting to fish these waters can register with any of the regional fishery boards (addresses later on in this appendix) and can thus fish all the Board's waters in all districts for £5 a year (1983).

Much trout water is controlled by clubs or private individuals and usually permits to fish these are available at prices from £1 a day to £5 a day. The big limestone lakes of the west, including Corrib, Mask, Conn and Carra, are completely free. In general, permits are required mostly for waters in the mid and upper Shannon region.

Visiting anglers are always advised to get in touch with the Regional Fishery Board responsible for the area in which they plan to fish. The board will advise them precisely where they can fish, and will give many other helpful details and hints.

Boats and ghillies
Boats are available for hire at most of the better fisheries and they usually cost between £5 and £8 a day, without ghillie or engine. An engine costs about £5 a day. An average price for boat, engine and boatman would be somewhere between £20 and £25 a day.

White trout

Under the Fisheries Act, white trout are treated as salmon and the one licence allows you to fish for both species. In the Republic you require a licence to fish for white trout.

Having this licence does not entitle you to fish anywhere you want but only in such waters where white trout fishing is free. This includes some fine waters, such as Lough Currane in Kerry, but most white trout fisheries are privately-owned and require a permit to fish them.

The following are the current charges for white trout and salmon licences:

All districts, full season £15
All districts, seven days £5
Late season (July on) all districts £10
Single district, specified, full season £7
Single district, specified, late season (July on) £5

Those anglers holding a licence for the Foyle Fishery District can buy an all-district, full-season licence for £10 or the single district, specified, licence for £4. The Foyle Conservancy is a joint venture run by both the Republic of Ireland Government and the Northern Ireland Government.

Licences are available either from the relevant Regional Fisheries Boards, the Central Fisheries Board or selected tackle dealers, all of whom are listed here as follows:

Fisheries Boards

Central Fisheries Board
The Manager,
Central Fisheries Board,
The Weir Lodge,
Earl's Island,
Galway.
Tel: (091) 65548
or
Balnagowan House,
Mobhi Boreen,
Glasnevin,
Dublin 9.
Tel: (01) 379206

Regional Fisheries Boards

Eastern
The Manager,
Eastern Regional Fisheries Board,
Balnagowan House, Mobhi Boreen,
Glasnevin, Dublin 9.
Tel: (01) 379206

Southern
The Manager,
Southern Regional Fisheries Board,
12 Gladstone Street,
Clonmel, Co. Tipperary.
Tel: (052) 23624

South Western
The Manager,
South Western Regional
Fisheries Board,
Macroom,
Co. Cork.
Tel: Macroom 625

Shannon
The Manager,
Shannon Regional
Fisheries Board,
Thomond Weir,
Limerick.
Tel: (061) 55175

Western
The Manager,
Western Regional
Fisheries Board,
The Weir Lodge,
Earl's Island,
Galway.
Tel: (091) 65548

North Western
North Western Regional
Fisheries Board,
Ardnaree House,
Abbey Street,
Ballina,
Co. Mayo.
Tel: (096) 22623

Northern
The Manager,
North Regional
Fisheries Board,
College Street,
Ballyshannon,
Co. Donegal.
Tel: (072) 65435

Tackle Shops

County Carlow
M. O'Donoghue,
14 Castle Street,
Carlow.

Messrs. Tully's Sports Centre,
150 Tullow Street,
Carlow.

M. A. McCullagh,
Market Square,
Muine Bheag.

Byrne & Dawson Ltd.,
Main Street,
Tullow.

County Cavan
J. McMahon,
Supply Stores,
Belturbet.

Mr. Brian Mulligan,
Main Street,
Cootehill.

J. J. O'Reilly,
Main Street,
Cavan.

Magnet Sports Stores,
Town Hall Street,
Cavan.

John Donoghue,
22 Bridge Street,
Cavan.

County Clare
McKeogh's,
Ballina,
Killaloe.

Mr. T. McNamara,
Mountshannon.

Dressco Ltd.,
Unit 12/13,
Shannon Town Centre,
Shannon.

County Cork
Mr. J. O'Sullivan,
4 Patrick Street,
Fermoy.

Vickery & Co.,
Main Street,
Bantry.

Mr. J. O'Sullivan,
The Pier,
Courtmachsherry.

T. W. Murray & Co. Ltd.,
87 Patrick Street,
Cork.

Roche's Leisure Shop,
17 Patrick Street,
Cork.

The Tackle Shop,
6 Davitts Quay,
Cork.

Atkins & Co. Ltd.,
The Square,
Dunmanway.

Mrs. P. Twohig,
Strand Street,
Kanturk.

Mylie Murphy Ltd.,
The Garage,
Kinsale.

Mallow Sports Centre,
21 Bridge Street,
Mallow.

County Donegal
Messrs. D. McLaughlin,
7 West End,
Buncrana.

Pat Barrett,
Bundoran.

C. J. Doherty,
Main Street,
Donegal.

Mr. J. J. McCrossan,
Lower Main Street,
Letterkenny.

B. O'Neill,
Bridgend,
Lifford P.O.

Eamonn Martin,
The Border Shop,
Lifford.

County Dublin
Garnetts & Keegan Ltd.
31 Parliament Street,
Dublin 2.

J. W. Elvery & Co. Ltd.,
Suffolk Street,
Dublin 2.

A.B.C. Stores,
15 Mary's Abbey,
Dublin 1.

Moorkens Ltd.,
11 Upper Abbey Street,
Dublin 7.

Watts Bros. Ltd.,
18 Ormond Quay,
Dublin 7.

Rory's,
17a Temple Bar,
Dublin 2.

Angling & Sports Centre,
13 Main Street,
Blackrock.

Fishermans Wharf,
(Mick Macs),
8 Railway Road,
Dalkey.

Clinton's Ltd.,
Tackle & Gunsmiths,
Ballydowd,
Lucan.

County Galway
Messrs. T. Cheevers,
North Gate Street,
Athenry.

Galway City Sports,
(The Great Outdoors),
Eglinton Street,
Galway.

Freeney's,
High Street,
Galway.

Mr. Hugh Duffy,
5, Mainguard Street,
Galway.

T. Naughton & Sons Ltd.,
35 Shop Street,
Galway.

K. Duffy & Son,
Main Street,
Headford.

Keller Bros.,
Ballinasloe.

Keogh's Ltd.,
Main Street,
Oughterard.

Garry Kenny,
Palmerstown Stores,
Portumna.

Thomas Tuck,
Main Street,
Oughterard.

County Kerry
Moriarty,
Seaview,
Fenit.

Handy Stores,
Kenmare Place,
Killarney.

Mrs. M. O'Neill,
6 Plunkett Street,
Killarney.

Messrs. D. N. Foley,
2 Main Street,
Killarney.

Benner & Co.,
28 Bridge Street,
Tralee.

Henberry Sports,
50 Ashe Street,
Tralee.

Mrs. A. J. Huggard,
Angler's Rest,
Waterville.

County Kildare
P. Mulhall,
20 Emily Square,
Athy.

Paul Cullen,
Moore Street,
Monasterevan.

John Cahill,
Sallins Road,
Naas.

Patrick A. Fleming,
New Road,
Naas.

Newbridge Rod & Gun,
Henry Road,
Newbridge.

McWey,
Round Tower House,
Kildare.

County Kilkenny
J. O'Leary & Son,
Lr. Main Street,
Graiguenamanagh.

Michael McGrath,
3 Lr. Patrick Street,
Kilkenny.

Kilkenny Sports Scene,
1 Irishtown,
Kilkenny.

County Laois
Messrs. Lawlor,
The Square,
Durrow.

County Leitrim
Conroy,
Rooskey,
Carrick-on-Shannon.

Phil's Fishing Tackle,
Main Street,
Ballinamore.

The Creel,
Main Street,
Carrick-on-Shannon.

County Limerick
McMahon's Sports Shop,
Roches Street,
Limerick.

Limerick Sports Stores,
10 William Street,
Limerick.

Nestor Bros. Ltd.,
28 O'Connell Street,
Limerick.

County Longford
Denniston,
Central Stores,
Longford.

County Louth
Olraine Agencies,
Unit 13,
Abbey Shopping Centre,
West Street,
Drogheda.

R. Q. O'Neill Ltd.,
Earl Street,
Dundalk.

Emerald Sports,
Earl Street,
Dundalk.

Magee Sports,
Shopping Centre,
Dundalk.

County Mayo
Messrs. O'Connor,
Main Street,
Ballycastle.

John Walkin,
Tone Street,
Ballina.

V. Doherty,
Bridge Street,
Ballina.

William Coyle,
American Street,
Belmullet.

Angler's Lounge,
Lower Main Street,
Swinford.

J. J. O'Connor,
15 Spencer Street,
Castlebar.

Messrs. Staunton Sports Shop,
Main Street,
Castlebar.

Pat Quinn Tackle,
Main Street,
Castlebar.

County Meath
"Tomas" Murray,
Farrell Street,
Kells.

The Rod & Gun Sports Shop,
Abbeylands,
Navan.

Londis Ltd.,
39 Trimgate Street,
Navan.

County Monaghan
T. J. Hanberry,
3/4 Fermanagh Street,
Clones.

County Roscommon
W. T. Wynne,
Main Street,
Boyle.

C. J. Finn,
Main Street,
Roscommon.

County Offaly
M. Madden,
29 Main Street,
Birr.

T. Holt,
Main Street,
Edenderry.

J. Hiney,
Main Street,
Ferbane.

County Sligo
M. J. Creegan,
2/4 Main Street,
Ballymote.

F. Nelson & Sons Ltd.,
42 Castle Street,
Sligo.

Barton Smith Ltd.,
Hyde Bridge,
Sligo.

County Tipperary
O'Keeffe,
O. K. Garage,
New Street,
Carrick-on-Suir.

John Kavanagh,
Westgate,
Clonmel.

Sheahan's Stores,
66 Pearse Street,
Nenagh.

Mr. Ken Henderson,
Main Street,
Roscrea.

G. W. Kilroy,
The Mall,
Thurles.

County Waterford
Messrs. Morgan Carroll & Co.,
The Square,
Ballybricken,
Waterford.

O'Bowman & Sons,
6 Mary Street,
Dungarvan.

John Casey,
12 Main Street,
Dungarvan.

Mark's Fishing Tackle Store,
35 Parnell Street,
Waterford.

R. Barnett,
Main Street,
Tramore.

County Westmeath
O'Malley Fishing Tackle,
33 Dominick Street,
Mullingar.

Mr. J. Murray,
Mullingar Sports Centre,
Castle Street,
Mullingar.

Foy's Fishing Tackle,
33 Church Street,
Athlone.

Denis Connell Tackle,
Dublin Gate Street,
Athlone.

Sean Egan Tackle,
59 Connaught Street,
Athlone.

S.G.S. Marine,
Ballykernan,
Athlone.

County Wexford
Paddy Lennon,
26 Main Street,
Enniscorthy.

John Webb,
100 Main Street,
Gorey.

Peter Goggin,
56 South Street,
New Ross.

Jim Mooney & Co. Ltd.,
North Street,
New Ross.

George Bridges,
14 Selskar Street,
Wexford.

Michael Goggin,
34 N. Main St.,
Wexford.

County Wicklow
George O'Toole Ltd.,
Lr. Main Street / Bridge Street,
Arklow.

Record Irish Trout and Specimen Weights

White trout
14 lb. 3 oz., caught on May 15th, 1973, on Dooagh beach, Achill, County Mayo, by Dr. Eoin Bresnihan. Specimen weight 6 lb.

Brown trout (lake)
26 lb. 2 oz., caught on July 15th, 1894, in Lough Ennell, County Westmeath, by William Meares. Specimen weight 10 lb.

Brown trout (river)
20 lb., caught on February 22nd, 1957, in River Shannon at Corbally, by Major Hugh Place. Specimen weight 5 lb.

Note: There are no official records for rainbows in Ireland. However some very heavy fish have been caught, including one of over 13 lb. caught in the White Lake, County Westmeath.

Seasons for Trout and White Trout

Brown Trout

Although some waters can be fished from as early as February 15th, including the Boyne system and some western waters, as a general rule trout fishing starts almost everywhere on March 1st and continues right through to September 30th.

Most fisheries close their waters on September 30th but some, again such as the Boyne, halt on September 15th, while others, such as Lough Conn and many small western fisheries, stay open until October 12th.

If in doubt as to whether a particular water is open or not, contact the local Regional Fisheries Board or angling clubs or tackle shops.

In Northern Ireland, the season varies from February 1st on some waters (Lough Melvin) through to the end of December for rainbows.

White Trout

As white trout are classed legally as salmon in the Republic, they share the same opening and closing dates, which vary much from area to area.

For the sake of simplicity, the following list of opening and closing dates runs according to date — i.e. starting with the earliest.

January 1
Liffey
Garavogue River, Lough Gill, Bonet River
Bundrowes River (Lough Melvin, February 1)
Glenveagh System
Lennon System (including Lough Fern)
January 17
Waterville River and Kerry Inny
Behy River, Caragh River and Lake
River Laune, River Maine and Killarney Lakes

February 1
Rivers Glyde, Dee, Boyne, Dargle
Rivers Barrow, Nore, Suir, Cork Blackwater, Lee
River Ilen
River Shannon, south of Portumna and tributaries (except Feale) of
Shannon below Portumna
Kilcolgan River
River Corrib, Lough Corrib, Owenboliska, Connemara Systems
Clifden and Cleggan waters, Dawros, Culfin, Erriff, Delphi,
Belclare, Burrishoole, Achill waters, Owenduff, Owenmore,
Ballinglen, Moy System (except Palmerstown River), Easkey River,
Ballisodare River, Drumcliffe River, Grange River, Bunduff River,
Lough Melvin
February 2
Bracky River, Gweebarra River, Owenmarve River, Dungloe
Waters, Gweedore River, Clady River, Crolly River, Bedlam River,
Glenna River, Tullaghobegly River, Ray River, Swilly River, Mill
River
February 15
Rivers Bandon, Argideen
February 26
River Slaney
March 1
Feale, Geale and Cashen Rivers
Shannon Systems above Portumna
Eske Systems (Donegal), Inver (Eany Water), Oily River, Stragar
River, Glen River
Crana River
Finn River (Foyle)
Fane River
March 15
Owenavaragh (Courtown)
Kenmare Bay Rivers
March 17
Dunmanus Bay and Bantry Bay Rivers
Rivers Emlagh, Anascaul and Dingle and Ventry Harbour streams
April 1
Caherciveen Rivers (Carhan, Ferta, etc.)
Brandon Bay and Tralee Bay Rivers
Rivers Bunowen, Carrowniskey
Owenea, Owentocker
Culdaff River

May 1
Feoghanagh River
Owengarve River (Mulrany)
Glenamoy
June 1
Palmerstown River (Ballina)

Statutory Closing Dates for Sea Trout Fishing
Sea trout which are regarded as salmon in law are exempt from the
statutory closing date of August 31. The closing dates for sea trout
fishing are as follows:
August 31
Slaney (above junction with and including R. Bann)
September 15
Mattock, Nanny, Feale, Geale, Cashen, Smearlagh, Slaney (below
junction with R. Bann), R. Finn (Foyle)
September 30
Owenavaragh (Courtown)
Waterford coastal streams (Colligan, Mahon, Tay, etc.)
Cork Blackwater
Brandon and Tralee Bay streams
Feoghanagh
Cullenagh (Inagh)
Newport River, Beltra L.
Owenmore
Owenea River, Owentocker River
Glenveagh System (Lackagh River, Glen L., etc.)
Glyde and Dee Rivers
October 9
Eske System
Inver (Eany Water)
Oily River, Stragar River, Glen River
October 10
Ballinglen River
October 12
Dargle System
Broadmeadow Ward
Argideen River
Bantry Bay, Dunmanus Bay and Kenmare Rivers (Roughty, etc.)
Meelagh, Owvane, Coomhola, Glengarriff
Waterville System, Kerry Inny, Clonee, Caragh

Caherciveen and Glenbeigh waters
Killarney Lakes, Maine River, Inch and Dingle area rivers
Kilcolgan River
Owenboliska River, Crumlin River
Screebe, Inver, Furnace, Cashla and Lettermucknoo Fisheries,
Carraroe, Gorumna Rivers and Carna area
Gowla Fishery, Ballynahinch Fishery, Dohulla Fishery
Clifden and Cleggan areas
Dawros, Culfin, Owenglin and Erriff systems
Delphi,   Carrowniskey,   Bunowen,   Belclare,   Burrishoole,
Owengarve, Achill waters, Owenduff, Glenamoy, Palmerstown,
Easkey, Drumcliffe, Grange, Bracky, Gweebarra, Owenmarve,
Dungloe Lakes (The Rosses), Gweedora, Clady, Crolly, Bedlam,
Glenna, Tullaghobegly
Swilly, Fanad Peninsula waters, Mill River, Cranna River, Fane
River
October 20
Culdaff River

Other Irish Trout

Slob trout are brown trout which have adapted to brackish water in river estuaries. Fishing for them is highly localised.

Gillaroo are very local in Ireland, Lough Melvin being by far the most notable centre. A fish of rocky lakes, it is a brightly-coloured and hard-fighting trout, and a free taker of the fly.

Sonaghan are again very localised, Lough Melvin also being the centre. A shoaling trout, it prefers deep water and docs not grow to anything like the size of a brown trout, and, like the gillaroo, is a free riser in certain conditions.

Ferox trout are basically big cannibal trout which rarely if ever rise to a fly. They inhabit particularly the bigger lakes, Lough Mask being the most notable centre, and are caught by trolling.

Dollaghan are big migratory lake trout coming upriver from such lakes as Lough Neagh in Northern Ireland. Night fishing with wet-fly has become the accepted method of catching these very big fish, usually from July onwards.

Croneen are the southern equivalent of the Northern dollaghan, centred around the Shannon and its tributaries — big lake trout running upriver in late summer. Evening/night wet-fly fishing tactics are best.

Bibliography

The books here listed include all those from which I have gained some little knowledge; doubtless there are omissions which will surprise some. Basically each of these books had something in them which could be applied to the often unique character of Irish trout fishing.

Besides the books, mention must be made of those excellent magazines *Trout and Salmon*, *Trout Fisherman*, *Fly Fisherman* and many other periodicals. They are a constant and pleasurable source of interest and new material.

Angler in Ireland, The: W. Belton, 1834
Angler's Guide to Ireland, The: Irish Tourist Board, 1957
Angler's Guide to the Irish Fisheries, The: Corrigeen (J. Adams), 1924
Angler's Paradise, An: F. D. Barker, 1929
Angler's Entomology, An: J. R. Harris, 1952
Angling Diversions: A. Courtney Williams, 1954
Angling Excursions of Gregory Greendrake, The: 1832
Angling Holidays: G. W. Gedney, 1896
Angling in Ulster Waters: Anon, 1950
Angling Reminiscences: Francis Francis, 1887

British Caddis Flies: M. E. Mosely, 1939
Brown Trout Fishing in Ireland: Anon, 1961

Complete Fly-Fisher, The: edited by C. F. Walker, 1963
Complete Trout and Salmon Fisherman: 1978

Day Stolen for Sport: P. Geen, n.d.
Dick Walker's Trout Fishing: 1982
Dictionary of Trout Flies, A: A. Courtney Williams, 1949
Dry-fly Fisherman's Entomology: M. E. Mosely, 1921
Dry-Fly Man's Handbook, The: F. M. Halford, 1913

Duffer's Luck: S. Gwynn, 1924

Erne, Its Legends and Its Fly-Fishing: H. Newlands, 1851

Family Water Naturalist, The: H. Angel and P. Wolseley, 1982

Film of Memory: Shane Leslie, 1938
Fishing and Philandering: A. Mainwaring, n.d.
Fishing and Thinking: A. A. Luce, 1959
Fishing Catechism: A. R. F. Meysey-Thompson, 1905
Fishing: Fact or Fantasy?: G. D. Luard, 1947
Fishing Fortunes and Misfortunes: G. D. Luard, 1942
Fishing for Lake Trout: Conrad Voss Bark, 1972
Fishing for Sea Trout in Saltwater: R. Clapham, 1950
Fishing from Afar: S. Johnson, n.d.
Fishing Holidays: S. Gwynn, 1904
Fishing in Ireland: D. Warner, K. Linnane, P. Brown, 1980
Fishing in Ireland: P. Geen, 1905
Fishing Memories: R. Lake, 1934
Fly Fishing: Sir E. Grey, 1899
Fly-Fisher's Life, A: C. Ritz, 1959
Fly-Fishing in Ireland: T. J. Hanna
Free-lance Angler in Ireland, A: L. Gaffey, n.d.
Freshwater Game Angling: Irish Tourist Board, 1983
Freshwater Life of the British Isles, The: J. Clegg, 1965
From Tyrone to the Test: J. Dickie, 1947

Going Fishing: N. Farson, 1942
Green Memory: J. B. Drought, 1937
Guide to Freshwater Invertebrate Animals, A: T. T. Macan, 1959

Handbook of Artificial Flies for Salmon and Trout: Department of
    Agriculture and Fisheries, Dublin, 1902
Happy Fisherman, The: S. Gwynn, 1936
Holiday Fisherman, A: M. Headlam, 1934
How and Where to Fish in Ireland: Hi-Regan (J. J. Dunne), 1900

Irish Bogs: J. W. Seigne, 1928
Irish Sport of Yesterday: A. W. Long, 1922

Lake Flies and their Imitation: C. F. Walker, 1960
Life in Lakes and Rivers: T. T. Macan and E. B. Worthington, 1972
Life of the Sea Trout: G. H. Nall, 1930
Loch Fishing in Theory and Practice: R. C. Bridgett, 1924

Man May Fish, A: T. C. Kingsmill Moore, 1979
Modern Trout Fishing: W. Carter Platts, 1938
More Hunting Memories: T. H. Grattan Esmonde, 1930

Newly from the Sea: Sidney Spencer, 1968
Nymph Fishing for Chalk-Stream Trout: G. E. M. Skues, 1932
Nymph Fishing in Practice: O. Kite, 1963

Practice of Angling, The: O'Gorman, 1845
Pursuit of Stillwater Trout, The: B. Clarke, 1975

River Fishing for Sea Trout: F. W. Holiday, 1960
River Plants: S. M. Haslam, 1978
River to River: S. Gwynn, 1937

Salmon and Seatrout in Wild Places: S. Spencer, 1968
Salmon and Trout Angling: J. Adams, 1925
Salmon and Trout Fishing in Ireland: W. J. Matson, 1910
Salmonia: Sir H. Davy, 1828
Salmon Rivers of Ireland, The: A. Grimble, 1913
Sea Trout: C. Gammon, 1974
Sea Trout Fishing: R. C. Bridgett, 1922
Sea Trout Fishing: H. Falkus, 1982
Side-lines, Sidelights and Reflections: G. E. M. Skues, 1932
Sportsman in Ireland, The: Cosmopolite (R. Allan, 1849)
Sportsman Looks at Éire, A: J. B. Drought, n.d.
Stillwater Fly-Fishing: T. C. Ivens, 1961
Summer on the Test, A: J. W. Hills, 1924
Sunshine and the Dry Fly: J. W. Dunne, 1924

Trout, The: W. E. Frost and M. E. Brown, 1967
Trout and the Fly, The: B. Clarke and J. Goddard, 1980
Trout Fishing: H. D. Turing, 1935
Trout Fishing: W. Earl Hodgson, 1904
Trout Fishing from All Angles: E. Taverner, 1929
Trout Fishing Memories and Morals: H. T. Sheringham, 1920
Trout Flies for Irish Waters: M. Kennedy, n.d.
Trout Fly Recognition: J. Goddard, 1966
Trout Problems: H. D. Turing, 1948

Way of a Trout with a Fly, The: G. E. M. Skues, 1928
Way of a Man with a Trout, The: G. E. M. Skues, ed. D. Overfield, 1977
Wild Sports in Ireland: J. Bickerdyke, 1897
Wild Sports of the West: W. H. Maxwell, n.d.

Year of Liberty, A: W. Peard, 1867

Index

143